247 Property Tax Questions Answered

By

Arthur Weller

Publisher Details
This guide is published by Tax Portal Ltd. 3 Sanderson Close, Great Sankey, Warrington, Cheshire, WA5 3LN.

'247 Property Tax Questions Answered' – First published in June 2009. Second edition July 2010, Third edition May 2011. Fourth edition May 2012. Fifth edition April 2015. Sixth edition April 2016. Seventh edition April 2017. Eighth edition April 2018. Ninth edition March 2019. Tenth edition May 2020. Eleventh edition March 2021. Twelfth edition April 2022. Thirteenth Edition 2023. Fourteenth Edition 2024.

Copyright
The right of Arthur Weller and Tax Portal Ltd to be identified as the authors of this guide has been asserted in accordance with the Copyright, Designs and Patents Act 1988, England.

© 2009-2024 Arthur Weller and Tax Portal Ltd

A CIP Copy of this book is available from the British Library.

978-1-7394153-5-8

All rights reserved
All rights reserved. No part of this guide may be reproduced or transmitted in any form or by any means, electronically or mechanically, including photocopying, recording or any information storage or retrieval system, without prior permission in writing from the publisher.

Trademarks
Property Tax Portal, Tax Portal Ltd and other Tax Portal Ltd services/ products referenced in this guide are registered trademarks or trademarks of Tax Portal Ltd in the UK and/or other countries.

Disclaimer

This guide is produced for General guidance only, and professional advice should be sought before any decision is made. Individual circumstances can vary and therefore no responsibility can be accepted by the author, Arthur Weller, or the publisher Tax Portal Ltd, for any action taken, or any decision made to refrain from action, by any readers of this guide.

Tax rules and legislation are constantly changing.

Neither the author nor Tax Portal Ltd offer financial, legal or investment advice. If you require such advice then, we urge you to seek the opinion of an appropriate professional in the relevant field. We care about your success and therefore encourage you to take appropriate advice before you put any of your financial or other resources at risk. Don't forget, investment values can decrease as well as increase.

To the fullest extent permitted by law, Arthur Weller and Tax Portal Ltd do not accept liability for any direct, indirect, special, consequential or other losses or damages of whatsoever kind arising from using this guide.

The guide itself is provided 'as is' without express or implied warranty.

Arthur Weller and Tax Portal Ltd reserve the right to alter any part of this guide at any time without notice.

Contents

About Arthur Weller 13

1. What Expenses Can I Offset Against Rental Income? 16
2. Switch Property With Your Spouse 16
3. Can I Offset Property Losses Against Other Income? 16
4. Can I Offset The Cost Of Buying A Vehicle? 17
5. Can We Merge Our Portfolio And Split The Income? 17
6. Can I Offset Money Paid To The Tenant? 17
7. How Do I Handle General Portfolio Costs? 18
8. I Rent Storage. Can I Offset The Costs? 18
9. Look To Claim Costs As 'Revenue Costs'? 18
10. Can I Claim My Costs For Re-Mortgaging? 19
11. Are These Costs Of A 'Capital' Or 'Revenue' Nature? 19
12. Do I Need To Have Receipts? 20
13. Can Service Charges Be Deducted? 20
14. Can I Transfer The Property? 20
15. Can I Pay A Family Member To Manage My Property? 21
16. Can We Offset Our Cost? 21
17. Capital Expenses From Profits? 22
18. Should I Buy In Sole Or Joint Name? 22
19. Can I Pay Myself For The Time Spent Managing Property Business? 23
20. Are These Legitimate Expenses? 23
21. Repairs To Commercial Property 23
22. As Joint Tenants Are We Forced To Split The Income For Tax Purposes? 24
23. Tax Implications Of Making Overpayments To My Mortgage? 24
24. Tax On Rental Income 24
25. Signing Over A Property To A Child 25
26. What Is The Tax Position On Fees For Re-Mortgages? 25

27. Can I Still Claim Tax Relief? 25
28. Is There A Tax Liability? 25
29. Is This An Expense Or A Capital Charge? 26
30. Am I A Landlord Or Not? 26
31. Is This A Tax Deductible Expense? 26
32. How Far Back Will HMRC Go To Assess My Income Tax Liability? 27
33. What Time Period Is Required To Avoid An HMRC Challenge? 27
34. Can We Split The Rental Profit This Way? 27
35. Are These Modernisations Capital Or Revenue Costs? 28
36. Would Our Tax Liability Be Affected? 28
37. What Constitutes Repairs To The Property Or An Improvement? 28
38. Joint Ownership Or Gifting Properties - What Is The Best Option? 29
39. Can I Receive Rents If I Don't Own The Property? 29
40. Property Owned By A Minor - Can This Be Done? 29
41. Do I Need To Include This In My Self-Assessment Form? 30
42. Tenants-In-Common And Property - What Will Be The Tax Position? 30
43. Rental Income Losses – Can I Offset? 30
44. Is There A Requirement To Declare? 30
45. How Do We Formalise Future Profits Agreement? 31
46. What Can A Landlord Charge? 31
47. Do I Claim Running Expenses Monthly Or Yearly? 31
48. Can I Claim Back Pre-Letting Costs? 32
49. How Do We Express Our Tax Wishes? 32
50. Property Refinance Costs – What Is The Tax Position? 32
51. What Is The Best Tax Saving Remortgage In My Circumstances? 32
52. What Would Be The Tax Consequences? 33
53. Can I Claim These Expenses, And If So, When? 33
54. Is This Classed As Extra Income And Is It Taxable? 34
55. What's The Most Efficient Way To Manage This? 34

56.	My First Tax Return	34
57.	Is This Transaction Considered A Second Property Purchase?	34
58.	Will There Be Tax On The Transfer Of A House?	35
59.	Can I Use Form 17 To Split The Income 90:10?	35
60.	Can We Claim Tax Relief On The Monthly Interest?	36
61.	Does Stamp Duty Land Tax Apply?	36
62.	Is The Cost Of Extending The Lease Tax Deductible?	36
63.	Is The Transaction Considered A Second Property Purchase?	36
64.	Who Is Liable For The Tax On The Rental Income?	37
65.	Covenant Query	37
66.	Changing The Name Of My Trust - Any Tax Penalties?	37
67.	Can I Claim Capital Allowances On Already Converted Property?	37
68.	Is It Worth The Investment?	38
69.	Are Married Couples Treated As One Unit?	38
70.	Will I Have To Pay Stamp Duty Land Tax?	38
71.	Will Tax Be Payable Once We Move Out?	39
72.	What Is The Tax Position If My Daughter Lives In My Second Home Rent-Free?	39
73.	Transfer Of House Pursuant To Consent Order	39
74.	Can I Deduct Losses From Rental Income Already Received?	40
75.	Can You Deduct Pre-Letting Repairs From Rental Income?	40
76.	What Are The Tax Rules On Buying A Second Property?	40
77.	What Tax If I Transfer My Primary Residence Into A Property Company?	41
78.	What Do I Declare As My Rental Income?	41
79.	Is A Capital Allowances Adjustment Necessary?	41
80.	What Tax On The Sale Of The Newly Built House?	41
81.	Funding A Buy-To-Let Deposit	42
82.	When Can A Re-Mortgage Be Tax Deductible?	42
83.	Buying And Transferring House To Son	42
84.	Can I Claim Interest On The Additional Equity Property?	43

85.	Nominating My New Purchase	43
86.	Can A Company Gift Money From The Sale Of A Property?	43
87.	Change To Gas Central Heating: Revenue Or Capital?	44
88.	Company Or Privately Owned?	44
89.	Tax Relief For Replacing Like-For-Like Sheds?	44
90.	Can Transferring A Property Maximise Our Personal Allowances?	44
91.	Are Storage Costs An Allowable Expense?	45
92.	Changing Th Rental Income Split	45
93.	Can My Daughter Live Rent Free?	45
94.	Non 50:50 Rental Income Split?	45
95.	When Is Rental Income Taxable?	46
96.	Will I Be Prosecuted For Forgetting To Declare Rental Income?	46
97.	What Expenses Can I Claim On Tax Return?	46
98.	Can Costs Of Condemned Boiler Be Deducted?	47
99.	Any Tax If I Sell My Home?	49
100.	How Can We Transfer The Property?	49
101.	Can I Select Any Property As My PPR?	49
102.	Can I Offset Costs If I Have Lived In The Property?	50
103.	Can I Sell My Property Below Market Value?	50
104.	When Should We Gift Our Son a Property We Are Buying?	50
105.	Tax Implications, If Any, Of Selling Part Of My Garden?	51
106.	Do I Have To Live In It To Be Exempt From Tax?	51
107.	Do I Have More Than One PPR?	51
108.	How Long In A Property Before I Get PPR?	52
109.	Can I Defer Capital Gains Tax?	52
110.	What CGT Liability For Property That Is Partly PPR?	52
111.	Can I Increase Borrowing To Minimise Or Avoid CGT?	53
112.	Do I Pay CGT If I Build Apartments In My Residence?	53
113.	Will I Be Able To Avoid CGT By Helping My Brother?	53

114. Is There CGT Due On A Property Purchased For My Mother?..................54

115. Can I Buy Property For A Child Under The Age Of 18?............................54

116. Can I Use Remainder Of My CGT Allowance?..54

117. Can I Claim Unused CGT For Previous Years?.......................................55

118. Can I Transfer My CGT Allowance?..55

119. How Can My Partner Reduce CGT?..55

120. What Is The Tax Date For CGT Purposes?...55

121. How Do I Work Out Capital Gains Tax (CGT)?..56

122. If We Sell At A Loss, Will We Still Have To Pay CGT?.............................56

123. Is There A Capital Gains Risk And/or An Offset?....................................56

124. Will This Avoid CGT?...57

125. Should I Move Into Previously Rented Out Property?.............................57

126. Can I Give A Family Member A Financial Gift?..57

127. How Do You 'Gift A Property In Stages'?...58

128. Avoiding Tax When Splitting A Property..58

129. Tax Treatment For New And Replacement Kitchens...............................58

130. What Tax If I Immediately Sell An Inherited Property?............................59

131. How Is Property Ownership Determined?...59

132. Can My Brother Discount His Share Of Property?..................................60

133. What Tax Will I Pay On A Transferred Property?....................................60

134. What Is The Tax Position On Transfers?...60

135. Would I Have To Pay Capital Gains Tax?..61

136. Which Valuation Figure Would Be Used?..61

137. Will There Be A Capital Gains Tax Liability?...61

138. Do I Pay Tax On What I Won't Receive?...62

139. Can I Minimise Capital Gains Tax?..62

140. Would We Be Liable For Capital Gains Tax?...62

141. Do I Need Receipts To Claim Against Capital Gains Tax?......................63

142. Can I Contest The Valuation?..63

143. How Can We Manage The Separation/Divorce Split? 63

144. Gifting Property Over Seven Years 64

145. Would I Have To Pay Additional Tax? 64

146. Will Essential Repair Costs Reduce My Tax Liability? 64

147. If I Sell My Only Home Would I Be Liable To Tax? 65

148. How Can We Transfer The Property And Not Pay Tax? 65

149. Gift Of Property With Mortgage 65

150. Tax Position for a Donor and Donee? 66

151. Passing Second Home Down the Generations 66

152. Can We Transfer Properties? 66

153. Gifting A Property To My Children 67

154. Tax Position On Selling Our Jointly Owned House 67

155. What If The Developer Pays More Than Market Value? 67

156. What Is My Tax Position On The Property Sale? 68

157. Will HMRC Think My Offer Is Illegal? 68

158. Tax Implications Of Gifting Property Or Cash 68

159. What Tax Implications If I Sign My House Over To My Daughter? 69

160. Splitting Title And Selling: What's The Best Thing To Do? 69

161. When Will Capital Gains Tax Be Calculated From? 70

162. What Is My Tax Position? 70

163. Tenant Wants To Purchase The Property 70

164. Selling My Home And Moving In With My Husband 71

165. Removing A Name From Property Title Deeds 71

166. Can Dad Sell A Mortgaged Flat To Me? 71

167. Putting My Current Properties Into A New Company? 72

168. Splitting Title And Selling: What's Should I Do? 72

169. When Will Capital Gains Tax Be Calculated From? 72

170. Can I Sell One Of My Properties At Less Than Cost? 73

171. Tax Position If He Gifts Me His Buy To Let Property? 73

172. Selling A Property We Haven't Occupied...73

173. Transferring Beneficial Ownership In A Flat..74

174. How Can I Minimise CGT On The Sale Of A Flat?...74

175. Is CGT Payable On A Deposit?..75

176. Any Tax Liability If Removed From Mortgage?..75

177. How Much Principal Private Residence Relief Can I Claim?...................................75

178. The Tax Position When Gifting Mortgaged Properties...76

179. Changing Houses: What Taxes?..76

180. Splitting Our Home Into Flats: What Tax Liability Will Arise?..................................76

181. Overseas Owner Of UK Property: The Tax Position On Selling...............................77

182. Transferring The Family Home From Single To Joint Siblings.................................77

183. Do I Set Any Selling And Capital Work Costs Against Tax?....................................78

184. What Are Our Tax Positions On Gifting Money For A Property?..............................78

185. Is There A Capital Gains Tax Liability On This Property Sale?................................78

186. Can We Estimate Costs In The Absence Of Receipts?...79

187. Sale Of Property To Tenant: How Do I Work Out The Capital Gains Tax?...............79

188. When Should I Nominate My Main Residence?..79

189. How Can He Avoid Capital Gains Tax On The Gifts Of Leases?.............................80

190. My Son Wants To Buy My House Tax Efficiently...80

191. When Does CGT Kick In: At Assignment Price Or Selling Price?............................80

192. Sell Both Properties As A Job Lot Or Separately?..80

193. Paying Half Of My Parent's House Purchase..81

194. Can I Offset A Loss In My Self-Assessment?..81

195. Which Valuation Report Should Be Used?..81

196. Transfer Of Benefit From Properties To Partner..82

197. Can Product Fees Be Capitalised?..82

198. Transferring Property In Stages By Trust...82

199. Selling Residential Property And Buying Another...83

200. Sell Both Properties As A Job Lot Or Separately?..83

201. What Would Be The CGT Position If We Pooled Our Property Resources? 83
202. Moving Out And Removing My Name From The Mortgage 84
203. Are Any Taxes Due When We Sell Our Principal Home? 84
204. Do We Need To Report No Capital Gains Tax Due? 84
205. What If I Move Into My Buy-To-Let Property And Then Sell? 84
206. CGT On Disposal Of Gifted Property: Which Price Do I Use? 85
207. When Selling Our Flat, Where Is The 'Factorial' Deducted From? 85
208. Taxed On Sale Of The Whole Property Or Just A Quarter Share? 85
209. When Will I Be Exempt From Paying CGT On Disposal Of My Property? 86
210. Tax Implications Of A Parent Transferring A Property Interest 86
211. Tax Implications Of Gifting Property To A Son 86
212. Are Costs of Extending A Lease An Allowable Expense? 87
213. What Are The Tax Implications Of Transferring Legal Title To My Property? 87
214. Purchase Lease Option And Minimising Tax Liabilities 88
215. What Would Be The Most Tax-Efficient Way Of Disposing Of Half A Property? 88
216. CGT Relief On Extending A Lease? 89
217. Sale Of Second Home: What Is The CGT Position? 89
218. Owner-Occupied For Part Of Ownership Period 89
219. Will I Have To Pay Capital Gains Tax? 90
220. Gift Of Property: What Base Cost Should I Use? 90
221. What Are The Tax Implications If Half Of The Property Is Transferred Into My Name?. 90
222. Should The Property Be Transferred To Me? 91
223. What Taxes Will Be Payable On Gifted Property? 91
224. How Can We Minimise Our Tax Liabilities When We Sell? 92
225. Boiler Change – Improvement for CGT purposes? 92
226. Any Tax If I gift My Share Of Property To Sibling? 93
227. Tax Implications Of Equity Transfer? 93
228. Renovating And Selling Our Home: What Is The Tax Position? 94
229. The Most Tax-Efficient Way To Transfer Equity 94

230. Can Lease Renewal Costs Be Claimed? 94

232. Inheritance Tax Planning - Which Is The Best Way? 96

233. Is There A Tax Efficient Way To Make Gifts? 96

234. How Do I Minimise My Children's IHT On A Property? 96

235. Using Property Gifted To My Son? 97

236. Can My Mother Live Rent-Free? 97

237. If I Die Will IHT Be Due Immediately? 98

238. How Can I Avoid Inheritance Tax? 98

239. What Is The Tax Position For A Settlor And Trustee? 98

240. Transferring Property From Sole To Joint Ownership - Any Pitfalls? 99

241. Mum Gave Me Gift Of House But Died Within Seven Years 99

242. Would Rented-Out Property Be Classed As PPR For IHT Purposes? 99

243. What Are The Tax Implications?? 100

244. Have We Left Ourselves Exposed to IHT? 100

245. Can I Gift Sale Proceeds To My Wife? 100

246. Transfer Of Mother's Home: Any Inheritance Tax (IHT) Pitfalls? 100

247. Transferring beneficial interest: What is the tax position? 101

About Arthur Weller

Arthur Weller is a tax specialist who advises other accountants. He is one of the most knowledgeable and respected tax specialists in the country. He is also the lead technical tax specialist and design consultant for www.property-tax-portal.co.uk.

Arthur is based in the northwest and qualified in 1997 as a certified accountant in a small firm of accountants. They specialised to a degree in property, and he worked for some years in their tax department.

He then moved on to a medium-sized firm, where he was the technical manager in the tax department.

In 1998 he passed the exams of the Institute of Taxation, and in June 2000 he left to set up his own tax consultancy.

Arthur works mainly in an advisory capacity for accountants in all areas of taxation. He also runs a telephone help line, giving phone advice on all areas of taxation to accountants around the country.

Much of his work has been focused in the following areas:

- property taxation (Arthur is regarded as a property tax specialist);
- capital gains tax;
- stamp duty;
- income tax;
- company tax.

Arthur also provides tax expertise to the following businesses:

landlord vision	**Landlord Vision** Landlord software solution that runs in the cloud. Try For FREE today. Visit: www.landlordvision.co.uk
tax insider	**Tax Insider** A website providing monthly tax newsletters to help UK taxpayers minimise their taxes. Visit: www.taxinsider.co.uk

Income Tax

1. **What Expenses Can I Offset Against Rental Income?**

   Question: I have just purchased my first buy-to-let property and have managed to successfully let it out. However, I am unsure as to what expenses I can offset against my rental income.

   Answer: Remember the golden rule: If you have incurred a revenue expense for the purpose of your property, then you can offset it against the rental income.

   This means that you can continue to lower your tax bill - *legitimately*. Most investors are aware that they can offset mortgage interest, insurance costs, rates, costs of decorating/repairs, wages and costs of services. Note new rules for mortgage interest from 6 April 2017.

   However, so many investors fail to claim the following costs, which when added together can provide a significant tax saving:

   - Costs incurred when travelling back-and-to the investment property.
   - Advertisement costs.
   - Telephone calls made (or text messages sent) in connection with the property
   - Cost of safety certificates.
   - Cost of bank charges (i.e. overdraft). But note new rules from 6 April 2017.
   - Advisory fees e.g. legal and accountancy.
   - Subscription to property investment related magazines, products and services.

2. **Switch Property With Your Spouse**

   Question: My husband works full-time and I have the more difficult job of looking after the home and children yet receive no income. Would it be better for me to own the property in my name?

   Answer: If you have a spouse who is a lower rate (or even nil rate) taxpayer and you are a higher rate taxpayer, then consider moving the greater portion of the property ownership into their name. This means that a greater part of the profit will be attributed to the lower (or nil rate) taxpayer thus meaning that any tax liability could be significantly reduced.

   This is a very powerful strategy if your spouse does not work, as any tax liability can be legitimately wiped out. Please note that in order to use this strategy you partner must be trustworthy as legally they will 'own' a greater share of the property.

3. **Can I Offset Property Losses Against Other Income?**

   Question: I have bought a property to let out and it is possible that in the first, and perhaps the second, year I will make a loss after accounting for insurances, mortgage interest and loan interest used to get a deposit. Can I offset that loss against my earnings from employment during the same period? If so which IR form do I need to use?

   Answer: The answer is 'no'. The losses cannot be offset against your employment income. However, they can be carried forward and offset against future rental income profits that are generated from the property business.

If you have been making losses, then it is important that you register those losses with the HMRC. The reason for this is because any losses can be carried forward and offset against future profits. For example, if in one tax year you made a £1,000 loss and then the following year you made a £1,000 profit, there is no tax liability as the £1,000 loss has been carried forward and wipes out your future gain!

However, if you have any other properties that are being rented out in the same tax year at a profit, then the loss from the loss-making property can be set off against the profit from the profit-making property.

4. Can I Offset The Cost Of Buying A Vehicle?

Question: Is it possible to offset the cost of buying a vehicle for use in your letting business, and if so, what would be the best way of doing this?

Answer: Here is a quote from the Revenue manuals page PIM2220:

Capital expenditure on providing the means to travel (usually a car or van) isn't deductible in computing rental business profits; nor is a depreciation charge. But plant and machinery capital allowances may be available. These allowances are deducted in computing the business profit or loss. The 'wholly and exclusively' rule applies to these allowances but, as with revenue expenditure, the landlord can claim the business proportion of the allowances. Plant and machinery allowances on cars costing more than £12,000 are also further restricted.

5. Can We Merge Our Portfolio And Split The Income?

Question: My Partner (life) and I operate 3 BTL's. She owns 1 and we jointly own 2. When completing tax-returns can we merge all 3 and split 50/50?

Answer: If the first property is solely in her name and not in joint ownership, it cannot be merged with the other two properties and must be attributed only to her. The remaining two properties, assuming they are 50-50 owned, can be split 50-50 for income tax purposes.

6. Can I Offset Money Paid To The Tenant?

Question: Having bought an investment property with a sitting tenant paying a low rent, I paid the tenant £20,000 to vacate and have now rented the property to a new tenant for 10 years at a much higher rent. Can I claim this premium as an expense against rental income or only as capital expenditure once the property is sold?

Answer: Firstly, from the High Court case Wateys London Ltd. v Pike (1982) quoted by the HMRC's Business Income Manual page BIM35545, it can be seen that this is capital expenditure, not revenue.

Secondly, in order to be allowable expenditure to offset against the sale proceeds when the property is sold, as enhancement expenditure under TCGA 1992 sec 38 paragraph 1(b), it must be reflected in the state or nature of the asset at the date of disposal (HMRC Capital Gains Tax Manual page CG15180).

Page CG71262 there says that if, after obtaining vacant possession, the landlord granted a new lease on essentially the same terms, the benefit would not be there at the date of disposal, and therefore the expenditure would not be allowable.

However, in this case, the new rent is much higher, so, by implication, this payment to the old tenant should be an allowable capital expenditure when the property is sold.

7. How Do I Handle General Portfolio Costs?

Question: I have a number of properties but some costs are generic and cannot be attributed to a single property. Is it possible to offset a cost against a single property or do I need to apportion them? For example, I purchased some decoration materials for painting and decorating two of my properties. Can I just offset the cost against one property?

Answer: In any tax year, all income and expenses from all the properties owned and rented out by a landlord operating a Schedule A property rental business are amalgamated and combined into one single account – for tax purposes. So, the answer to your question is that as long as the cost is attributed to the correct tax year in which it occurred, it doesn't make a difference which property it was for.

8. I Rent Storage. Can I Offset The Costs?

Question: I have some flats on rental. Sometimes I have to remove furniture from a flat because the tenant does not like a particular piece. I therefore rent storage space in which I keep a supply of items of furniture which move into and out of any one of up to 7 flats. Can the rental charges be placed against my income in the same way as other (allowable) expenses?

Answer: Yes, the cost of renting storage space is allowable. The reason is that it fulfils the principal criteria of 'wholly and exclusively', as the cost was incurred for the purpose of your property business. If you had never rented property, then you would not be incurring such costs.

Case Study:

> John owns 5 properties which are all fully furnished. However, he finds a new long-term tenant for his property who has his own furniture and furnishings. John decides that he will empty the property and store the furniture in rented storage. The cost of rental storage is £450. This amount can be offset against the rental income as it has been incurred 'wholly and exclusively' for the purpose of the rental business.

9. Look To Claim Costs As 'Revenue Costs'?

Question: I have been advised to always try to claim costs as 'Revenue Costs' wherever possible. Why should I do this?

Answer: The simple reason is that it improves your cash flow and means that you do not have to wait until you dispose of the property before you can claim the expense. By claiming it is a 'Revenue Cost' you can offset it against your annual rental income, which means that ultimately you could be paying little or no income tax.

10. Can I Claim My Costs For Re-Mortgaging?

Question: I have heard that mortgage broker and mortgage lender fees are of a revenue nature and valuation costs are of a capital nature. Is this also true if an investment property is re-mortgaged? I am about to re-mortgage an investment property with a different lender and will incur these costs again, but am unsure if I can claim relief against them.

Answer: The answer is that it depends on the status of the interest on the loan. If the interest on the loan is an allowable expense, the cost of obtaining the loan is also an allowable expense. So, in this particular instance, because the loan that is being re-mortgaged is for the purpose of the property then once again the costs can be offset. See HMRC Business Income Manual page BIM45815 (no.8 in the list).

Again, the mortgage broker and mortgage lender fees will be claimed against your rental income, and the valuation costs will be claimed once you decide to sell the property.

Case Study:

> John has a buy-to-let mortgage with an outstanding amount of £50,000. He is currently repaying £450 per calendar month back to the bank. However, he realizes that another lender has a special reduced interest rate, so if he re-mortgages with them his monthly rate will be reduced to £400.
>
> He re-mortgages the property and incurs costs as follows:
>
> Mortgage broker fees £250
> Mortgage lender fees £200
> Survey costs £200
>
> This means he can offset £450 against his annual rental income and can claim the survey costs when he decides to sell the property.

11. Are These Costs Of A 'Capital' Or 'Revenue' Nature?

Question: Could you please clarify whether the following costs are deemed to be 'capital' or 'revenue'.

- Mortgage broker fees i.e. I have paid a mortgage broker a % arrangement fee
- Mortgage lenders arrangement fee
- Property valuation costs

Answer: The Property Income Manual page PIM2105 says: 'Costs you incur in obtaining loan finance for your rental business are generally deductible in computing rental business profits provided they relate wholly and exclusively to property let out on a commercial basis.

These costs include loan fees, commissions, guarantee fees and fees in connection with the security of a loan.'

This means that a) and b) are classed as revenue expenditures and can therefore be offset against the rental income.

Property valuation costs are dependent on the purpose for which the valuation was obtained. If for the purpose of buying or selling the property, then they will be capital costs. If for insurance purposes, or for the purposes of obtaining loan finance, then they will be revenue expenses. See the Revenue manuals pages PIM2120 and BIM45815 (no.3 in the list).

So, to summarize, a) and b) are Revenue Costs and can be offset against your annual rental income and c) is a dependent on the purpose for which the valuation was obtained.

12. **Do I Need To Have Receipts?**

   Question: Do you have to have receipts in order to claim property related expenditures? What happens if you do not have a receipt or have lost them?

   Answer: If you know in your heart that you did spend the money on an allowable expense, then you can claim it. However, if the HMRC question you about it and you cannot prove it, then you must be prepared for the HMRC to say to you: 'We don't believe you and therefore we are not accepting what you say'.

   Thus, although you are allowed to claim it because you know it is true, you must be prepared to pay the tax on it if questioned about it whilst being unable to prove it.

13. **Can Service Charges Be Deducted?**

   Question: Can all service charges and building Improvements carried out by a Leasehold Management Company be deducted as a cost from the rental income of a Buy-to-Let property?

   Answer: All service charges can be deducted. Building improvements can be deducted if they are revenue expenses but not if they are capital expenses. It is not easy to distinguish between the two but, in a nutshell, revenue expenses are small repairs and general upkeep, like painting and 'like for like' replacements, whereas capital expenses are extensions, big repairs and replacements that are a major upgrade from the original.

14. **Can I Transfer The Property?**

   Question: I am currently looking into transferring a rental property into my wife's name in order to take advantage of her personal tax allowance, half of which she is not using. This could mean the majority of our rental income (about £4,000 a year) would be tax free.

   I understand that I do not have to transfer any legal ownership to my wife, but I will need a declaration of trust. Can I transfer 100 per cent of the property income to my wife and, if so, will all paperwork (bills etc.) relating to the property need to be in my wife's name?

   I have made an appointment to see a tax adviser as I am aware that I need to do this properly, and, like most tax matters, it is a little more complicated than I originally thought.

Answer: What you have written is correct. The beneficial ownership needs to be transferred to your wife, and this can be done by a declaration of trust. If you transfer 100% of the property to your wife, then you will succeed in transferring 100% of the property income to her. All the paperwork relating to the property should be in your wife's name.

15. Can I Pay A Family Member To Manage My Property?

Question: I have a property in my hometown and live elsewhere. It is currently for sale but being rented whilst trying to sell.

Rather than pay a mortgage company to be on call, can I pay any other family member a nominal monthly fee to be on call for any problems, emergencies, etc. so long as it is similar or less in price than an agency would charge for an equivalent service?

Answer: You can pay a family member to do the job you would have asked an agency to do, and pay them the normal price for the job as long as it is equivalent to a normal commercial arrangement. Make sure regular payments are made from your bank account into a bank account in their name and that the amounts you pay them are reasonable. And that they actually do the job!

16. Can We Offset Our Cost?

Question: My wife & I own a flat that we use occasionally at weekends when we visit our hometown in Liverpool. We live in rented accommodation in the south of England due to current work commitments. We plan to rent the flat out on a short-term basis (per night) that will allow us to still have occasional use, and in this tax year we would expect to get around +/- 90 nights of rent.

Can we offset the costs i.e. mortgage, council tax and service charges of the flat for the full tax year against income tax on this rent?

We understand that any use of the flat by ourselves would be deducted from any tax relief.

Answer: Here is a quote from the Revenue Property Income Manual page PIM2052 about interest payments but the same applies to mortgage, council tax and service charges:

'A property may be let for short periods in a tax year or only part of it may be let throughout a tax year (or both); the rest of the time the property is used for private or non-business purposes. Here the interest charged on a qualifying loan on that property has to be split between the rental business use and the private or non-business use. The split is done in whatever way produces a fair and reasonable business deduction, taking account of both the proportion of business use and the length of business use.

You don't have to split the interest if the taxpayer is genuinely trying to let the property but it is empty because they have not been able to find a tenant. In this case the interest will meet the 'wholly and exclusively' test. It won't meet this test if they have not been trying to let the property or they have been using it for private or non-business purposes.'

17. Capital Expenses From Profits?

Question: Tax law states that you can deduct from the profit you have from the sale of a rental property anything you have done to enhance its value (but not repairs and maintenance). HM Revenue & Customs (HMRC) gives the example of an extension. My question is: can I deduct the cost of installing central heating, a new bathroom and a new kitchen?

Answer: In one sentence, the answer to your question is that you can claim the cost of installing central heating, a new bathroom and a new kitchen if a) you did not previously claim these costs as revenue expenditure against your rental income, and b) the new installations were a considerable improvement over the corresponding heating, bathroom and kitchen that were in the property before.

Here is a quote from the HMRC, talking about claiming the cost of installing a new kitchen as a repair, against rental income:

'For example, if a fitted kitchen is refurbished the type of work carried out might include the stripping out and replacement of base units, wall units, sink etc., re-tiling, work top replacement, repairs to floor coverings and associated re-plastering and re-wiring. Provided the kitchen is replaced with a similar standard kitchen then this is a repair and the expenditure is allowable.

If at the same time additional cabinets are fitted, increasing the storage space, or extra equipment is installed, then this element is a capital addition and not allowable (applying whatever apportionment basis is reasonable on the facts).

But if the whole kitchen is substantially upgraded, for example if standard units are replaced by expensive customised items using high quality materials, the whole expenditure will be capital.'

18. Should I Buy In Sole Or Joint Name?

Question: I am trying to work out what my options are if I/we buy a property to do up and sell on using the equity from our main residence. The question is whether to buy in just my name or in joint names with my husband and, in this particular case, would income be subject to CGT or income tax if we did manage to sell? If we do not manage to sell, my contingency plan would be to rent the property out for a period of time. I am currently not working though if this project succeeds, I might consider future developments. My husband and I currently rent out a property which was our main residence many years ago and is jointly owned and my husband is a 40% taxpayer.

Answer: If you buy a property, do it up and sell on, the profits would be subject to income tax, because this is a trading venture. If you rent out the property, you will be in receipt of rental income, which again is subject to income tax.

In light of the fact that you currently do not work, which I presume means that you have little or no income, but your husband is a 40% taxpayer, it would seem the best option for you to buy only in your name so that any profits will be subject to your marginal rate of income tax i.e. 20% and not your husband's rate of 40%.

However, you need to consider the effect of buying in your own name, and not in joint names, on the possibility of getting a loan to do the project and the rate of interest you pay your lender, and, if you decide to take out a joint loan, whether you can offset all of the interest against your personal business venture.

19. Can I Pay Myself For The Time Spent Managing Property Business?

Question: I live and run my UK properties from Cyprus. I find that I am spending a lot of time keeping my portfolio up to date, for which I am not being paid. If I was a tax resident of the UK, regardless of whether I paid myself for looking after the rental properties or not, I would still need to declare my worldwide income and be taxed accordingly. This is a 'catch 22' situation but as I am a tax resident of Cyprus, I only need to declare my UK income to the UK tax authorities. Therefore, if I pay myself in Cyprus for the work I carry out here with regards to my UK properties, can I then claim this on my tax returns? Obviously, I would then have to declare this to my own tax authority and be taxed accordingly but the tax relief bracket is higher here so less tax would have to be paid.

Answer: On page PIM2210 of HMRC's Property Income Manual (www.gov.uk/hmrc-internal-manuals/property-income-manual/pim2210), it states:

'A landlord can't deduct anything for the time they spend themselves working in their own rental business.'

So even though you put time and effort into your property business, you cannot put a monetary value on that time and effort and claim it as an allowable business expense, under UK property tax rules.

20. Are These Legitimate Expenses?

Question: We purchased four buy to let properties during 09-10. Each one needed decorating and re carpeting prior to letting to make them clean and habitable. We had one boiler condemned and replaced and had to make electrics safe prior to occupation. Are these legitimate expenses to set against our tax liability for 2015-16?

Answer: If you look on the HMRC website on the Property Income Manual pages PIM2030 & PIM2505:

www.gov.uk/hmrc-internal-manuals/property-income-manual/pim2030
www.hmrc.gov.uk/manuals/pimmanual/PIM2505.htm

You will see that if the property was in a fit state to rent out when you purchased it and the purchase price was not significantly reduced due to the property being in a bad state, then any standard 'repairs and renewals' that would be allowable against rental income in the middle of tenancy are similarly allowable before the first tenancy begins.

21. Repairs To Commercial Property

Question: If a business rents a commercial property and has to replace part of the concrete floor in the warehouse to enable continued operations. Would this be an allowable expense?

Answer: If I understand you correctly, you are a tenant who runs a business from premises that you rent from a landlord, and you have to pay for the repair of the concrete floor. Your question is: is this payment an allowable business, revenue, expense that you can offset in full in the current year against your business profits? If you look on the HMRC Property Income Manual you can see that a repair of a part of the structure of a property, when the replacement can be classified as 'like for like', i.e. without a significant upgrade or improvement to what was there originally, can be treated as a revenue, allowable business expense. This can be true even if the repairs are substantial.

22. As Joint Tenants Are We Forced To Split The Income For Tax Purposes?

Question: My wife and I own a property as Joint Tenants as opposed to Tenants in Common. Due to our respective incomes, it would be more advantageous if we could apportion all of the income to my wife.

Answer: In order to achieve what you want, i.e. more of the rental income to be taxed in your wife's name, you need to do two things. Firstly, you need to transfer a corresponding proportion of the property into your wife's name, either by formal conveyance, or by deed of trust to transfer beneficial ownership. Secondly within 60 days you need to complete a Form 17 (www.hmrc.gov.uk/forms/form17.pdf) and send it into HMRC together with proof of the transfer. The result of this will be your being taxed according to the actual proportion of the ownership, and not on a 50:50 basis.

23. Tax Implications Of Making Overpayments To My Mortgage?

Question: I would like to know what the tax implications are on making regular overpayments and/or 'lump sum' overpayments to pay off the capital on a 'buy to let' interest only mortgage.

Will I have to pay extra tax using this method if I were to use the 'excess monthly rent' as monthly overpayments once the monthly mortgage has been paid?

Answer: The answer to your question is very simple. Any interest payment you make to your mortgage lender is an allowable expense that can be offset against your gross rental income for calculating income tax.

Any capital repayment you make is not an allowable expense, and so cannot be offset against the gross rental income. Your mortgage lender should be able to tell you which payments you make are classified as interest payments and which are classified as capital repayments.

From April 2017, new rules have become effective for a residential property landlord claiming relief for interest paid to a lender.

24. Tax On Rental Income

Question: Can I classify the total monthly mortgage repayment against total monthly rental, or only the interest element?

Answer: Only the interest element of the total monthly mortgage repayment can be treated as an allowable business expense to offset against your gross rental income. The remainder is a capital expense that reduces the original debt that you owe the lender, and is not relevant to your rental business.

From April 2017, there are new rules for a residential property landlord claiming relief for interest paid to a lender.

25. Signing Over A Property To A Child

Question: What age does a child need to be for a parent to sign their property over them?

Answer: A child under the age of 18 cannot be a legal owner of property in this country. However, they can have beneficial ownership, which is really what counts. So, you can sign over beneficial ownership of a property to a child of any age, but if they are under 18, an adult will have to own it in trust for the child, the adult's name will have to be on the legal documents, and you will need a deed of trust to show the child's beneficial ownership.

26. What Is The Tax Position On Fees For Re-Mortgages?

Question: I am re-mortgaging one of my buy-to-let properties, which incurs fees for the lender and the conveyancer. Are they in any way tax deductible?

Answer: You are re-mortgaging one of your buy to let properties, which incurs fees. I think you mean to say, this incurs fees for the borrower. If you look on page PIM2066 in the Property Income Manual on HMRC website (www.gov.uk/hmrc-internal-manuals/business-income-manual/bim45815) you can see that incidental costs incurred in obtaining loan finance, like arrangement fees, are allowable. So, if the loan is allowable, which I presume it is, the fees incurred in setting up the loan are also allowable.

27. Can I Still Claim Tax Relief?

Question: I moved out of my residential property and took out an interest only buy to let mortgage and let out the property. After approximately 8 years I have moved back into the property (although I still have a second residence). Can I still claim the tax relief on the interest on the buy to let mortgage? Can I rent the property to myself to claim any tax relief?

Answer: Firstly, you cannot rent the property to yourself. Secondly, tax relief on the interest you pay your lender is only available to reduce your taxable rental income – if you have no rental income, it cannot be reduced. The interest you pay your lender cannot be offset against any other taxable income. From April 2017 there are new rules for interest paid by a residential landlord.

28. Is There A Tax Liability?

Question: I took a loan of my mortgage and invested the money elsewhere to get higher rate of interest. To explain with an example, I took withdrew £60,000 from my mortgage and put this money in a savings account which gives me 3% AER while my mortgage is 0.98%. Now I have to pay 0.98% on £60,000 to my bank. Do I pay tax on the difference? I.e. 3% less 0.98% or the entire 3% because I am paying interest (0.98%) on the loan anyway?

Answer: You are not a money lender running a money lending business, but an individual investor. Therefore, you pay tax on the entire 3%, but the 0.98% is not an allowable expense to offset against the 3%.

29. Is This An Expense Or A Capital Charge?

Question: We have a property in the UK which is rented to students. Due to the nature of the type of tenant, the tenants tend to change each year. Is it right that the expense charged by our managing agents for drawing up this agreement cannot be charged as an expense, but rather as a capital charge? We have been renting out this property for 12 years on this basis so it's hardly a new enterprise.

Answer: If you look at www.gov.uk/hmrc-internal-manuals/property-income-manual/pim2120 you can see that if the let is for a year or less, then the legal expenses (such as the cost of drawing up a lease) and the agent's fees are not capital expenditure, and are therefore an allowable revenue expense.

30. Am I A Landlord Or Not?

Question: My wife and I jointly own my mother-in-law's flat which we inherited in 2005. In her will, the asset was to be shared also with my wife's brother and sister. By re-mortgaging (interest only) my present house I raised the funds to buy out the brother and sister. My wife and I now jointly own the flat with no mortgage and I have a mortgage on our home which is solely in my name. Since gaining ownership of the flat we have only ever let it, first to our son for several years and then to our daughter who is claiming housing benefit. We have never charged a commercial rent as the intention was to help them out. I have never declared this second property to HMRC. My mortgage comes to an end next year. What are my risks and liabilities and your advice for mitigating them please?

Answer: If you have received rental income from a property that you own, whether at a commercial rate or below it, then you are obligated to inform HMRC. The exception to this rule is in a situation when both of the following conditions apply: a) You are not liable to tax on the rental income, either because the amount is covered by your income tax personal allowance (you don't have other income using up your personal allowance); or because your allowable expenses on the property equal or exceed the rent. b) Your gross rental income (before deducting allowable expenses) is less than £10,000 per annum, and your net rental income is less than £2,500 per annum. See: www.gov.uk/self-assessment-tax-returns/who-must-send-a-tax-return.

If you look back over your records from the past years and you find that you owe tax to HMRC, then the best thing is for you to approach them first, before they approach you.

31. Is This A Tax Deductible Expense?

Question: I have a really old bathroom in my let property, over 15 years old. I want to take it out and install a new bathroom for the new tenants, totally decorate and upgrade. Is this tax deductible?

Answer: Here is a quote from HMRC's property income manual ('Even if the repairs are substantial, that does not of itself make them capital for tax purposes, provided the character of the asset remains unchanged. For example, if a fitted kitchen is refurbished the type of work carried out might include the stripping out and replacement of base units, wall units, sink etc., re-tiling, work top replacement, repairs to floor coverings and associated re-plastering and re-wiring.

Provided the kitchen is replaced with a similar standard kitchen then this is a repair and the expenditure is allowable. If at the same time additional cabinets are fitted, increasing the storage space, or extra equipment is installed, then this element is a capital addition and not allowable (applying whatever apportionment basis is reasonable on the facts).

But if the whole kitchen is substantially upgraded, for example if standard units are replaced by expensive customised items using high quality materials, the whole expenditure will be capital. There is no longer any relief for 'notional repairs', which is the notional cost of the repairs that would otherwise have had to be carried out.'

32. How Far Back Will HMRC Go To Assess My Income Tax Liability?

Question: I have been renting out a property for about 8 years through a letting agency. I assumed that the letting agency was dealing with the tax aspects and so never sent in an income tax return. I recently became aware that I should send in a tax return and would like to know how far back the HMRC will want to assess my income.

Answer: The first thing is to make a calculation for each of the last 8 tax years separately to see whether a) you have actually made a net profit from your rental business (i.e. that your rental income is more than your allowable expenses), and b) that those profits are subject to tax (e.g. they are not covered by personal allowances or brought forward rental losses). If, after these calculations, you find that you owe tax to HMRC then your best option is to contact HMRC (before they contact you!) on the voluntary disclosure helpline on 0300 123 1078.

33. What Time Period Is Required To Avoid An HMRC Challenge?

Question: What time period needs to elapse between the transfer and sale of a property to avoid an HMRC challenge? In our case, we wish to sell my wife's investment property but use my annual capital gains tax CGT allowance and some of my rolled forward capital losses.

Answer: Strictly speaking, HMRC does not like 'asset splitting'; see www.gov.uk/hmrc-internal-manuals/capital-gains-manual/cg18150). However, in practice many people do it. There is no minimum period that needs to elapse between transfer and sale to avoid an HMRC challenge. Perhaps some people would say: (a) 6 months; others would say (b) do the two things in separate tax years; and others would say (c) something different.

34. Can We Split The Rental Profit This Way?

Question: My wife, son and I have just purchased a property in Scotland in our joint names - one-third each. My wife and I only wish to cover our interest on the loan that we have taken out to purchase the property, with our son receiving the balance of the rental profit. Is it possible to do this?

Answer: Assuming your son is over 18, yes, it is possible to do so. Draw up a written income agreement saying that even though the ownership of the property is one third each, nevertheless the income is entitled to be received in a different proportion. Then make sure that the right amount of income actually goes to a single name bank account for that individual. The taxation will follow the entitlement to the rental income, as per the agreement.

35. Are These Modernisations Capital Or Revenue Costs?

Question: I have recently bought a property that has needed full modernisation – double-glazed windows, carpets, bathroom, kitchen, painting, boiler replacement, etc. Is this all treated as a capital cost as it is pre-tenancy or can it be treated as a revenue expense? Tenants will move in the day after the work is completed.

Answer: Look at www.gov.uk/hmrc-internal-manuals/property-income-manual/pim2030 where you can see that the crucial questions to ask are: a) was the property not in a fit state for rental use before the refurbishment was carried out? or b) was the price paid for the property substantially reduced because of its dilapidated state? If yes, then the refurbishment costs are capital expenditure.

36. Would Our Tax Liability Be Affected?

Question: We will soon be renting out our residential property due to moving overseas for work. I know that the interest only part of our mortgage payment attracts tax relief, but if we put some or all of the remaining rental income into an offset or overpayment account with our mortgage provider, would that affect our tax liability?

Answer: This is a quote from a lending bank: 'An offset mortgage links your current and savings account balances to your mortgage in order to reduce the mortgage balance you're charged interest on. So, if your mortgage balance is £125,000 and you have £25,000 in your linked current and savings accounts, we'd calculate your monthly mortgage interest on £100,000 instead of the full mortgage balance of £125,000.

You can use the offset savings in one of two ways: (1) Reduce your mortgage payments. The interest you save in one month by offsetting could reduce your mortgage payment the following month. (2) Reduce your mortgage term. Keep your monthly mortgage payments the same and pay off your mortgage sooner.' I

If you choose the first option, and consequently make smaller monthly interest payments, your net taxable profit will consequently be larger, so your tax bill should be higher. But there are other factors to take into account, e.g. whether you are eligible for a UK income tax personal allowance, and how much is your total UK income.

37. What Constitutes Repairs To The Property Or An Improvement?

Question: I have a receipt from a tradesman who did some work for me in my rented-out property. The receipt says 'remove and dispose of existing bathroom. Replace bathroom with shower and small bathroom fittings.' There was a bath originally and the room itself a bit dated. The bath has been replaced with a shower and made more presentable to help with re-letting the property.

Answer: If you look at HMRC's Property Income manual (at www.gov.uk/hmrc-internal-manuals/property-income-manual/pim2030), you can see how HMRC distinguishes between an improvement and a replacement of 'like for like'. From what you have described it would seem that your case is a revenue expense, allowable against rental income.

38. Joint Ownership Or Gifting Properties - What Is The Best Option?

Question: My wife (lower rate taxpayer) and I (higher rate taxpayer) are looking at buying a few more buy-to-let properties. Our eldest daughter is 18; the other two are under 18. Is it beneficial for these new properties to be in my wife, eldest daughter and my name? Would this split the profits three ways? What about the other two children - should we do anything now or wait until they become 18?

Answer: It is a good idea to make all five family members own a share of the property now. However, any income attributable to those under 18 will be taxed on the parents. Between the three over 18, you could draw up a written income agreement giving more income to your daughter (i.e. a bigger percentage share of the income than her share of ownership of the property). This will enable the rental income to be taxed at lower rates (presumably she has little other income) and will also perhaps help to support her at this stage of her life (e.g. through university).

39. Can I Receive Rents If I Don't Own The Property?

Question: Can my rental property be gifted to my child and the rental benefits still be paid to myself for my lifetime?

Answer: You can certainly gift your rental property to your child. But the rental income will belong to them, and they will pay income tax on its receipt; see HMRC's Trusts and Estates manual at www.gov.uk/hmrc-internal-manuals/trusts-settlements-and-estates-manual/tsem9310. If afterwards they choose to gift to you the money they receive from renting out the property, that is a purely a gift from them to you.

40. Property Owned By A Minor - Can This Be Done?

Question: I co-own a business. We recently transferred the business from an LLP to a company. I have a director's account in my company, but once that is exhausted I'll be a higher rate taxpayer again. We are accumulating capital in the business (about £300,000 last time I looked). We have bought all the kit we need for the business and cleared all loans. I now want to start investing in property to rent out, and to hold for years while the value climbs (as it seems to be starting to again). My business partner and I might do this as a company project, but for the time being his personal circumstances mean he doesn't want to complicate his 'share' of the business with property.

I could take out £120,000 to buy a property for rental and I've seen one that would be ideal. My son is 14 and in private education and I have the following questions: (1) Can I buy this property in his name (my wife and I as legal owners, son as beneficial owner)? (2) Can rental revenue then be paid into an account in his name to minimise the tax burden? (3) Can that account then be used to pay his school fees?

Answer: You can certainly buy the property with you and your wife the legal owners and your son as the beneficial owner. However, due to the 'settlements' anti-avoidance legislation, annual income from any asset owned by an unmarried minor bought by the parents' capital is taxed, for income tax purposes, on the parents, if the annual income is more than £100 per parent per tax year. But maybe it is still worth it for you because when he becomes 18 this rule won't apply any more.

41. Do I Need To Include This In My Self-Assessment Form?

Question: If one owns a property jointly and it is not being let at present, but is occupied by a family member who pays the outgoings, does one still have to inform the tax office on one's return? And can one of the joint owners be elected as the owner responsible for declaring income when it is let in the future?

Answer: If in a tax year you do not receive any rental income you do not need to inform HM Revenue & Customs on a tax return. If joint owners receive rental income from a property (e.g. four people receive a quarter each), then each one is responsible for declaring his quarter on his own tax return - one of the joint owners cannot be made responsible to declare on behalf of all of them.

42. Tenants-In-Common And Property - What Will Be The Tax Position?

Question: My husband and I held our house as tenants-in-common. He died in 1988 and left his share to our daughter. I now wish to sell the house and move nearer to my daughter; she lives 100 miles away. Will she have to pay any tax on the sale?

Answer: Yes, she will have to pay capital gains tax on her half of the house, based on the difference between the value in 1988 when she inherited from her father, and today's sale proceeds. I am making an assumption that she never lived in the house as her principal private residence after acquiring her half in 1988, because if she did, then that changes the picture considerably.

43. Rental Income Losses – Can I Offset?

Question: I realise that such losses can normally only be offset against profits on rented property. However, what is the position if I sell the property I rent out, but there are remaining losses which I therefore cannot offset in the future? Can I then offset these against my income, which is all from pensions or do I simply have to forget this loss?

Answer: In HMRC's Property Income manual at www.hmrc.gov.uk/manuals/pimmanual/PIM4210.htm it explains, like you said, that rental losses can only be set against profits from the same rental business. If that rental business ceases, the losses cannot be used. However, if you look at www.hmrc.gov.uk/manuals/pimmanual/PIM2510.htm you can see the rules for cessation of a rental business. For example, if at the time this rental property is sold the taxpayer still owns another property that they are actively trying to rent out then this rental business has not ceased.

44. Is There A Requirement To Declare?

Question: If I set up a property company and have the rent paid directly into the company and don't have the rental money paid to me directly, do I still have to personally declare this rental income held in the company in my self-assessment form for the year the rent money is paid into the company?

Answer: If you are the legal landlord, and therefore legally entitled to the rental income, it won't help to divert the rental income to a company, you will still be taxable on it. However, if you rent out the property to the company and allow the company to sublet the property to a third-party tenant, then the rent paid by the tenant to the company will only be assessable on the company. The advantage of this arrangement is that you can charge your company a small rent, perhaps equal to your expenses, and your company can charge the tenant the commercial rent (a much higher figure), so that the real profit is made in the company.

45. How Do We Formalise Future Profits Agreement?

Question: Our situation is that we purchased a flat as a home for our son, thus both listed on the Land Registry and Mortgage Loan. Our son has subsequently moved abroad and the flat has been let under permission to let. The flat is managed by a letting agency who pay income into our son's bank account and from which the mortgage payments are made. We gain no share of profits. We are seeking to reallocate future profits from the default 50:50 to (say) 90:10 in favour of our son (our son having the lower income tax liability). Please advise how this is best formalised and if this has to be notified to HMRC.

Answer: Draw up a written agreement between yourself and son saying that even though the flat is owned 50:50 nevertheless the entitlement to the rental income is going to be in the proportion 90:10, and is actually going to be received 90:10. Then make sure that 90% of the rental income goes into a bank account in his sole name. This agreement does not need to be notified to HMRC unless they question you.

46. What Can A Landlord Charge?

Question: What charge can I, as a landlord, make in terms of calculating for work I've done such as painting instead of employing a painter?

Answer: Unfortunately, it says on www.gov.uk/hmrc-internal-manuals/property-income-manual/pim2210: 'A landlord can't deduct anything for the time they spend themselves working in their own rental business' (it says something similar regarding capital expenditure at www.hmrc.gov.uk/manuals/cgmanual/CG15210.htm). A deduction can, of course, be made for the expense of materials purchased.

47. Do I Claim Running Expenses Monthly Or Yearly?

Question: I'm thinking of renting my house and am looking at tax issues. With regard to running expenses, can I claim these monthly or yearly? I know I have to do a tax return once a year, is it the same for claiming expenses?

Answer: The tax year for property rental runs from 6 April to 5 April. You need to put together all the rental income in this period, and all the allowable expenses in this period, and put the figures once a year on the self-assessment supplementary pages for UK property. See www.gov.uk/government/publications/self-assessment-uk-property-sa105 . See www.hmrc.gov.uk/manuals/pimmanual/PIM1101.htm, which explains the dates that rental income is taxable, and the dates that rental expenses can be offset against rental income.

48. Can I Claim Back Pre-Letting Costs?

Question: I am thinking of letting out my house as a self-catering holiday property and moving to the country. What tax would I have to pay on the income? Can I claim back any work needing doing to the property against the tax?

Answer: The simple answer is that income tax would apply to your net rental income. If the conditions of your scenario comply with the furnished holiday lettings rules (see www.gov.uk/government/publications/furnished-holiday-lettings-hs253-self-assessment-helpsheet/hs253-furnished-holiday-lettings-2017) then slightly different income tax rules apply. If the property is currently in a fit state to rent out, and any refurbishment work you do is not an improvement (see www.hmrc.gov.uk/manuals/pimmanual/PIM2020.htm), then the cost can be offset against the rental income.

49. How Do We Express Our Tax Wishes?

Question: Our house in multiple occupation (HMO) is going to incur large losses in the first year, and these can be claimed back through sideways loss relief. We have been told that my husband can claim solely for this (he is a higher rate taxpayer) and rental income going forward can be in my name only (I pay basic rate). We have also been told we do not need to complete a declaration of trust, as we can just write a letter to each other expressing our wishes. This seems too easy!

Answer: If I understand you correctly, your husband is claiming all the losses sideways (see www.hmrc.gov.uk/manuals/pimmanual/PIM4220.htm) because he is currently the sole owner of the HMO. The intention is that all future rental income profits will be yours only; this can only be if he transfers 100% of the beneficial ownership of the property to you. In order to do this, you will need a written declaration of trust – (see www.hmrc.gov.uk/manuals/tsemmanual/TSEM9520.htm).

50. Property Refinance Costs – What Is The Tax Position?

Question: How are property refinance costs treated for tax purposes? Specifically, legal fees, search fees and new lender's fees. On the original purchase, of course all these costs are not allowable for current income purposes, but form part of any eventual capital gains computation.

Answer: On original purchase, legal fees, search fees and other fees relating to the purchase are classified as capital expenditure - see www.gov.uk/hmrc-internal-manuals/property-income-manual/pim2120. But fees relating to obtaining loan finance are allowable revenue expenses - see www.gov.uk/hmrc-internal-manuals/property-income-manual/pim2105. If the refinance simply replaces and stands in the shoes of the original finance, then the refinance fees should also be allowed, like the original. See www.gov.uk/hmrc-internal-manuals/business-income-manual/bim45815..

51. What Is The Best Tax Saving Remortgage In My Circumstances?

Question: I am employed on a £60,000 salary. On the top of that, I have £20,000 rental income. One buy-to-let (BTL) mortgage is repayment and the other is interest only. I set off both interest on both mortgages against my income, as well as repairs, ground rent, etc. It is time to re-mortgage the interest only mortgage, and I don't know if I would be better off by doing interest only but increasing the monthly payments so it matches my income and don't have profit to pay tax on, or if I change it to repayment so I can pay it off quickly. I have more than double equity on this property so the other thought would be to withdraw some equity to invest in another BTL.

Answer: The government have brought in new rules that apply from April 2017 to restrict the amount of interest that can be offset against rental income. This will affect you because you are a higher rate taxpayer. If you have the option, you are best off paying off your mortgages as quickly as possible.

52. What Would Be The Tax Consequences?

Question: We are looking to buy our next property but the current property, which we bought using a 'Help To Buy' equity loan, is not having many viewings. To help us, our in-laws have offered to buy the property with cash at the original purchase price so that we can be chain-free and not incur the second home stamp duty land tax (SDLT) supplement (as there is a very real chance of completing on the next property before we have sold this one). Is it legal to sell the property to them at the original purchase price or even at a lower price and are there any tax consequences for any of the parties?

Answer: It is certainly legal to sell the property to them at the original purchase price, or even at a lower price, but for capital gains tax purposes it is deemed that you are selling to them at today's market value. See www.gov.uk/hmrc-internal-manuals/capital-gains-manual/cg14530. This should not cause you a problem, because I would imagine that any capital gain you incur by this sale is covered by principal private residence relief (PPR).

However, I would suggest you think twice about this arrangement because your in-laws will have to pay SDLT on the purchase of the house from you, based on the amount they actually pay you. Furthermore, according to the new rules, if you only sell your current main residence after purchase of a new main residence, as long as it is within three years, you can get a refund of the extra 3% SDLT. See www.gov.uk/government/uploads/system/uploads/attachment_data/file/570876/SDLT_Higher_rates_for_additional_properties.pdf at section 3.25.

53. Can I Claim These Expenses, And If So, When?

Question: I recently purchased a modest terraced property last updated in the 1970's. I have replaced the kitchen, upgraded the wiring and decorated and re-floored throughout. We now have a tenant moving in. We intend to replace the bathroom (1970's style again) and also need to replace some rotten windows in the sun porch once the tenant is living there. Can we do these shortly after the tenant moves in and claim the works as expenses against tax, or do we need to leave a set period before doing this? Am I right in assuming that we cannot claim against tax the refurbishment we did prior to the tenant moving in?

Answer: Look at www.gov.uk/hmrc-internal-manuals/property-income-manual/pim2020, where you can see a distinction made between improvements, and like-for-like replacements. The former costs are called capital expenditure, and can only be offset against the capital gain when the property is sold. The latter costs are called revenue expenditure. If the property was in a fit state to rent out before your refurbishment, all the revenue expenditure can be set off against rental income, whenever you do it, even before the tenant moves in.

54. Is This Classed As Extra Income And Is It Taxable?

Question: I own a property with my partner in the UK but I work and live in the Channel Islands. I pay her half of the mortgage payments every month into her bank account, and she in turn pays our lender. Is this classed as extra income for her, and is she obliged to declare the source to HMRC?

Answer: If you can show from her bank statements that the money you pay into her account equals the money she pays out to the lender on your behalf, on a regular basis, then you should be okay. But besides that, it cannot be classed as extra income for her, because she does not work for you.

55. What's The Most Efficient Way To Manage This?

Question: My wife and I have recently bought a small property with our savings. We intend to let it out, but first it requires some work (kitchen, bathroom, complete decoration, etc.). For some work, like roof repairs and electrical works I will pay professionals, and offset that against expenses. Most of the other work I will carry out myself. I've planned for it to take me four months. I'm currently unemployed, hence the project. I would like to know whether, if I'm drawing on savings to support us and pay the home bills, could this be seen as income; would I end up paying basic rate, or can I offset it against capital gains when and if we decide to sell? I just wondered the most efficient way to manage this.

Answer: Firstly, drawing on savings is not considered income, so there is no tax liability on such withdrawals. Secondly, your own labour on your own investment asset is also not considered income. Thirdly, your own labour is not an allowable expense, both for rental income tax purposes (see www.hmrc.gov.uk/manuals/pimmanual/PIM2080.htm) and also for capital gains tax purposes (see www.hmrc.gov.uk/manuals/cgmanual/CG15210.htm).

56. My First Tax Return

Question: When making the first tax return on a rented property, can I offset the deposit, the solicitor's fee and the stamp duty against tax?

Answer: I presume the 'deposit' means the first payment for the purchase of the house. These three items relate to the purchase of the house and are therefore considered to be 'capital expenses'. They cannot be entered on the first tax return for a rented property, to offset against rental income. Instead, when the property is eventually sold they should be entered on the capital gains supplementary pages of the tax return, to be offset against the capital gain. See HMRC's guidance here: www.gov.uk/hmrc-internal-manuals/capital-gains-manual/cg15250.

57. Is This Transaction Considered A Second Property Purchase?

Question: If I buy a flat in London that is connected to mine in order to join the two back together into the original configuration of the house (for which I already own the freehold), is that transaction considered as a second property for stamp duty land tax (SDLT) purposes? If I complete the transaction and merge the titles on the same day, does that make any difference?

Answer: It would seem to me that you would have to pay the extra 3% SDLT. See HMRC's guidance at www.gov.uk/government/uploads/system/uploads/attachment_data/file/570876/SDLT_Higher_rates_for_additional_properties.pdF. In section 3.7, it states that one of the conditions for paying the extra 3% is Condition C 'the individual purchaser owns, or is treated as owning, a major interest in another dwelling'. In section 3.12, it states: 'The interest held at the end of the day must be an interest in another dwelling. A further interest owned in the same dwelling in which a major interest has been purchased will not, on its own, cause Condition C to be met.' But in section 2.10A, it states: 'A self-contained part of a building will be a separate dwelling if the residents of that part can live independently of the residents of the rest of the building including independent access and domestic facilities.'

58. Will There Be Tax On The Transfer Of A House?

Question: Twenty-five years ago, my mum put part of a down payment on my house. I was going through a divorce. The monies came from injury compensation prior to marriage, but I was worried he would take it. The house stayed in mum's name all these years. I made payments to her and she retained the loan. She wants to sign it over to me now. Can I retain the current tax base and do I have to pay huge taxes on it? There is a lot of equity. The loan is still in her name; my name is not on it. My brother thinks the house should be in her trust to be divided. My mum wants me to have the house. I'm partially disabled and I have no money to pay taxes on the equity. I'm getting conflicting advice.

Answer: There is a possibility to argue that your mother was purely a legal owner, nominee or bare trustee of the house, but you had the beneficial ownership all along. Because some of the original funds to purchase the house came from you, and you occupied the house all the time. See www.gov.uk/hmrc-internal-manuals/capital-gains-manual/cg70230. If so, transferring the house from her legal ownership to yours will have no tax consequences. See www.gov.uk/hmrc-internal-manuals/capital-gains-manual/cg10720. You can strengthen this argument by your mother now writing a declaration of trust, saying that from the beginning she has held this property on trust for you, see www.gov.uk/hmrc-internal-manuals/capital-gains-manual/cg65406. However, it must be stated that HMRC may challenge this argument.

59. Can I Use Form 17 To Split The Income 90:10?

Question: I have two properties in my sole name and am a 40% taxpayer, whereas my wife has no income at all. I am looking to enter her on the deed by transferring her 50% of the equity on these properties. She will be hit with a tax bill of £3,750 on £125,000, but we okay are with this. Can I then use Form 17 to split the income 90:10 in her favour?

Answer: You can use the Form 17 to transfer 90% of the income to her. But you first need to actually transfer 90% of the house to her, and then submit the Form 17 within 60 days of the transfer. See www.gov.uk/hmrc-internal-manuals/trusts-settlements-and-estates-manual/tsem9800, in particular TSEM9850. In order to achieve this, you don't need to first transfer 50% to her.

60. Can We Claim Tax Relief On The Monthly Interest?

Question: Our daughter lives in our buy-to-let property and no rent is paid to us. We pay the monthly interest. Are we entitled to any tax relief?

Answer: If you look at www.gov.uk/hmrc-internal-manuals/property-income-manual/pim2130 you can see that if a property is not let out at a commercial rent then the landlord cannot claim all the expenses. The landlord can only claim expenses up to the amount of rent received. If you are not receiving any rent from your daughter, you cannot claim any expenses.

61. Does Stamp Duty Land Tax Apply?

Question: My company has diversified into property rental and development, and has the opportunity to buy part of a garden in London which has no buildings on it or present access to it. I own the land that has the access to it. Does stamp duty land tax (SDLT) apply? The purchase price is £245,000.

Answer: This garden is a chargeable interest in land, for SDLT purposes www.gov.uk/hmrc-internal-manuals/stamp-duty-land-tax-manual/sdltm00280, and therefore SDLT will apply.

62. Is The Cost Of Extending The Lease Tax Deductible?

Question: I own a buy-to-let property and I have 85 years remaining on the lease. I understand that the cost of extending a lease (i.e. valuation, lawyers etc.) is tax deductible. However, I have also been informed that if a lease is extended for less than the statutory right, that cost of the lease is also tax deductible. Can you confirm this please?

Answer: If you look at HMRC's Property Income manual (www.gov.uk/hmrc-internal-manuals/property-income-manual/pim2205), you can see that you are correct, the costs of extending a lease are tax deductible; but only where the lease is for less than 50 years is it allowable against rental income, for the annual income tax computation. Otherwise, it is only allowable against the capital gain when the property is eventually sold, for the capital gains tax computation.

63. Is The Transaction Considered A Second Property Purchase?

Question: If I buy a flat in London that is connected to mine in order to join the two back together into the original configuration of the house (for which I already own the freehold), is that transaction considered as a second property for stamp duty land tax (SDLT) purposes? If I complete the transaction and merge the titles on the same day, does that make any difference?

Answer: It would seem to me that you would have to pay the extra 3% SDLT. See HMRC's guidance at: www.gov.uk/government/uploads/system/uploads/attachment_data/file/570876/SDLT_Higher_rates_for_additional_properties.pd. In section 3.7, it states that one of the conditions for paying the extra 3% is Condition C 'the individual purchaser owns, or is treated as owning, a major interest in another dwelling'. In section 3.12, it states: 'The interest held at the end of the day must be an interest in another dwelling. A further interest owned in the same dwelling in which a major interest has been purchased will not, on its own, cause Condition C to be met.' But in section 2.10A, it states: 'A self-contained part of a building will be a separate dwelling if the residents of that part can live independently of the residents of the rest of the building including independent access and domestic facilities.'

64. Who Is Liable For The Tax On The Rental Income?

Question: I am going to let my flat and want to pay the tax out of the rental income, but my father and stepmother are the legal owners of the flat I have been told that they are liable for the tax, even though the rental income will be coming to me. Is there a way that I can be responsible for the tax and avoid them having to pay it?

Answer: It sounds as though the flat is in the legal ownership of your father and stepmother, but you have the beneficial ownership. If so, you should establish this in writing, perhaps through a declaration of trust (note that this declaration of trust may have tax consequences - speak to a tax adviser). Once you have established that you have the beneficial ownership of the flat, then you are in receipt of the rental income, and you are responsible to pay the income tax on it. See HMRC guidance at: www.gov.uk/hmrc-internal-manuals/trusts-settlements-and-estates-manual/tsem9922.

65. Covenant Query

Question: I am selling land to a developer. There is a covenant that I have to pay. Is the covenant payment allowable against capital gains tax?

Answer: When someone sells land to a developer, sometimes the seller imposes a 'restrictive covenant' on the buyer. To do so can mean increased legal costs for the seller. If you look at HMRC's Capital Gains manual (at www.gov.uk/hmrc-internal-manuals/capital-gains-manual/cg15250 and www.gov.uk/hmrc-internal-manuals/capital-gains-manual/cg15280), you can see that these legal costs should be allowable as 'incidental costs', to reduce the capital gain.

66. Changing The Name Of My Trust - Any Tax Penalties?

Question: I have set up a trust and want to include my flat in London as part of it. In order to do so, I need to change the name on the deed from my own name to the name of my trust. Will this change involve any tax charges?

Answer: If I understand you correctly, you are transferring not only the legal ownership of the flat to the trust, but also the beneficial ownership (i.e. a full transfer). If so, the transfer will be subject to capital gains tax (CGT) and stamp duty land tax (SDLT). However, there may be no CGT or reduced CGT to pay if the flat was your main residence for all or part of your period of ownership, and the SDLT to pay will be based on the amount the trust pays you, so if a gift for no consideration - no SDLT.

67. Can I Claim Capital Allowances On Already Converted Property?

Question: I am about to purchase a property. Are capital allowances claimable on a property already converted into three self-contained flats?

Answer: Capital allowances are not due on the cost of houses, flats or other residential accommodation. Furthermore, plant and machinery capital allowances are not available on any furniture equipment supplied with residential furniture that is let furnished, except in the case of qualifying furnished holiday lettings (see www.gov.uk/hmrc-internal-manuals/property-income-manual/pim3020). However, there is a 'replacement of domestic items relief' potentially available for furnished lettings (see PIM3210. Additionally, there may be some scope for claiming capital allowances for expenditure on the 'common parts' of a block of flats, e.g. stairs and lifts (see: www.gov.uk/hmrc-internal-manuals/capital-allowances-manual/ca23060).

68. **Is It Worth The Investment?**

    Question: If a new build buy-to-let property investment in London just breaks even, is it still worth investing in for a potential capital gain in the next five years?

    Answer: This is not a tax question, rather an investment question. Having said that, you need to consider what else you could do with your money (opportunity cost) versus the potential five-year capital gain on this property, less the capital gains tax that will be payable when the property is sold (additionally, consider all the effort involved in renting out the property for five years, unless, perhaps, your 'break even' calculations assume a managing agent will have responsibility for renting out the property).

69. **Are Married Couples Treated As One Unit?**

    Question: I want to purchase a second property in Manchester for me and my wife to live in. However, I already own a property held jointly with my brother and which is currently rented out. Unfortunately, I am caught out by the stamp duty land tax (SDLT) rule changes introduced back in 2016, but want clarification if I will have only to pay half of the SDLT due on the purchase of another property. The second property will be purchased jointly with my wife (who does not own another property) and she will be on the title deeds as well as the mortgage deeds. Are married couples treated as one unit in regard to purchase of a second property and hence a liability to pay the SDLT?

    Answer: See www.gov.uk/hmrc-internal-manuals/stamp-duty-land-tax-manual/sdltm09820 and SDLTM09766 that the full extra 3% SDLT will apply to this purchase, because all the four conditions are fulfilled by you, and a married couple are looked upon, for these rules, as one unit (I presume that your interest in the first property is worth more than £40,000; see sdltm09780).

70. **Will I Have To Pay Stamp Duty Land Tax?**

    Question: I have a mortgage on my current residential home. However, I would like to purchase a new house to live in and leave the old one as a buy-to-let property. I would also like to leave it for my daughter for future security, but she is under-age at the moment. I presume I will fall foul of the extra stamp duty land tax (SDLT) on this second home even if it's going to be my live-in property?

    Answer: Your presumption that you will have to pay the extra 3% SDLT on this second home even if it is going is going to be your next main residence is correct. However, if you gave away your current main residence to someone else and then bought your new house to live in, you would not have to pay the extra 3%, even though you are not selling to them (see HMRC's SDLT manual at www.gov.uk/hmrc-internal-manuals/stamp-duty-land-tax-manual/sdltm09800). When your daughter becomes of age this person can give the house to your daughter. But you would have to find someone you trust; and there could be capital gains tax when this person transfers to your daughter, if the house has gone up in value. You also have to consider the receipt of the rental income while the house is in the possession of this person.

71. Will Tax Be Payable Once We Move Out?

Question: I have owned a buy-to-let property for four years. However I've recently re-mortgaged the buy-to-let property and realised that we might need to move in genuinely for a few years and move on to a bigger house later. After living in the property for one year and we move out, will I have to pay capital gains tax?

Answer: If the house genuinely becomes your principal private residence (PPR) then you will be exempt from capital gains tax on the eventual sale of the house for: (a) the one year period you actually lived in the house as your PPR; plus (b) the last 18 months of ownership (unless this overlaps with the one year); plus (c) you will be eligible for lettings relief for the period the house was rented out (unless it overlaps with the 18 months). The rest of the capital gain will be chargeable on you.

72. What Is The Tax Position If My Daughter Lives In My Second Home Rent-Free?

Question: I am looking to buy a second home in York; my daughter lives with me and cannot afford her own home yet. If I pay the mortgage on my current home, when I move and allow my daughter to live here what would be the tax implications for both of us? Would not having to pay rent to me be seen as a benefit and thus affect her tax allowance? Apart from second home tax, what other liability would I have if I let her live rent-free?

Answer: Your daughter not having to pay rent would not be seen as a benefit for tax purposes, and thus would not affect her tax allowance. By 'second home tax' I presume you mean the extra 3% stamp duty land tax when you buy the second home. But this has nothing to do with allowing her to live rent free in your first home. There is no other tax liability for you in allowing her to live rent free.

73. Transfer Of House Pursuant To Consent Order

Question: I currently own a house in Exeter with my ex-wife. I am transferring the property pursuant to a consent order into mine and my new girlfriend's name. My ex-wife is receiving a lump sum of money and we are repaying the existing mortgage and taking a new mortgage in our joint names. Am I liable to any stamp duty land tax?

Answer: If you look at www.gov.uk/hmrc-internal-manuals/stamp-duty-land-tax-manual/sdltm00550 you can see that certain transactions on the ending of a marriage are exempt from stamp duty land tax. These transactions are those made between the parties to the marriage as a result of:

- certain types of court order;
- an agreement between the spouses/partners in contemplation or in connection to the dissolution or annulment of their marriage or civil partnership; or

- their judicial separation or a separation order.

However, the exemption is not available if the transaction involves someone other than the spouses or civil partners. So, it is worth checking to see whether it makes a difference that the property is being transferred into the names of both you and your new girlfriend.

74. Can I Deduct Losses From Rental Income Already Received?

Question: If my overseas apartment is vacant and I cannot find a tenant, can the empty period be calculated as a loss as no income is coming due to its being vacant at the moment? Can I count the months it has been empty and deduct the empty period rental value from the period it generated rental income?

Answer: It is not clear what you mean in your question. But it seems to me that what you are asking is that where (for example) the usual rent is £1,000 per month, and the property is vacant for five months, whether you can deduct £5,000 from rental income that you earned during the time that the property was actually rented out (i.e. from the £7,000 actually earned), so that you only pay tax on £2,000? The answer is that you can't; the loss of £5,000 is not an actual allowable expense that can be deducted from income. It is just 'missing income'.

75. Can You Deduct Pre-Letting Repairs From Rental Income?

Question: Are repairs to a property carried out 3 or 4 years before the first rent is received be allowed for deduction against rental income? Are estate agents fees charged for an initial rental period of more than 1 year allowable against rents received?

Answer: If you look at HMRC's internal manual here: www.gov.uk/hmrc-internal-manuals/property-income-manual/pim2505 that per the rules written there, an expense incurred up to seven years before the first rent is received, is allowable. However this assumes that you were not living in the property yourself when the repairs were done. Also see there pim2120 where it says: 'The expenses incurred in connection with the first letting or subletting of a property for more than one year are capital expenditure and therefore not allowable. The expenses include, for example, legal expenses (such as the cost of drawing up the lease), agent's and surveyor's fees and commission. Expenses for a let of a year or less can be deducted.'

76. What Are The Tax Rules On Buying A Second Property?

Question: We are considering buying the flat above ours in Coventry and then joining them to make one large duplex flat. Would we be able to reclaim the additional stamp duty land tax charge (i.e. the extra 3% we would be paying for a second purchase)?

Answer: If you look at HMRC's Stamp Duty Land Tax manual at SDLTM09810 (https://tinyurl.com/5bajbsck at Example 9) you will see that in HMRC's view, this is considered to be the purchase of a second dwelling, and this is not a replacement of the main residence. A refund cannot be claimed once the two properties are merged because the original residence is still owned, albeit in an altered form.

77. What Tax If I Transfer My Primary Residence Into A Property Company?

Question: I want to transfer my primary residence in Leeds (the only home I own) into a new property company (a special purpose vehicle). What taxes are liable? I assume it's free of capital gains tax as it's my primary residence. I plan to move out of that home and rent it out in the next 18 months.

Answer: Firstly, you should transfer to the company after you move out of the property because if you live in the property while it belongs to the company, you will be receiving a benefit-in-kind, which will trigger income tax for you. The transfer itself will make the company liable to stamp duty land tax, based on the market value of the property. However, it is worth speaking to a tax adviser, who may find a way for you to achieve your objectives without having to actually transfer the property into the company (e.g. a 'rent-to-rent' arrangement).

78. What Do I Declare As My Rental Income?

Question: I receive rent via a letting agent; the agent takes out any maintenance costs etc. before they pay me the rent each month. Can you tell me whether I have to declare the original whole amount of rent to HMRC and then deduct the maintenance costs etc., or can I just enter the rental income as the amount I receive after maintenance deductions?

Answer: You need to declare the gross rent before any deductions, then all the allowable expenses, and then the net rent.

79. Is A Capital Allowances Adjustment Necessary?

Question: I've been renting out a furnished holiday let for three years now and have spent significant sums on capital expenditure. I've claimed these back as capital allowances. I've not made a profit on any of the three years trading and have significant accumulated losses. I now want to move into the furnished holiday let as my main residence and rent out my current house. What are the implications of doing this from a capital allowances point of view? Do I have to adjust my tax return for capital allowances/balancing charges for the year in which I do this?

Answer: If you look at HMRC's Property Income manual (at the end of www.gov.uk/hmrc-internal-manuals/property-income-manual/pim4110), you can see that when you start to occupy the property as your main residence, the property will stop being a qualifying furnished holiday letting, and you will have to work out any balancing allowance or balancing charge for capital allowances purposes. See HMRC's guidance in its Help Sheet HS252 at sections 7.7, 7.8 and 7.9.

80. What Tax On The Sale Of The Newly Built House?

Question: We are redeveloping our property and have planning permission to demolish the existing bungalow and replace it with two detached houses. We have to build both houses ourselves because there are complications with the site and we wish to avoid a prolonged construction period. What tax will be charged when we sell one of the new houses?

Answer: I presume that you intend to sell this new house when you complete it, or soon afterwards. If so, this is a 'trading transaction'. You are acting as property developers, so when you sell the house you have built, you will be subject to income tax on the profit you make, and Class 4 National insurance contributions may be payable as well. The construction industry scheme rules also need to be considered.

81. Funding A Buy-To-Let Deposit

Question: Is it possible or allowed to use cash from a personal loan to fund a deposit towards a buy-to-let (BTL) property?

Answer: It is possible or allowed to use cash from a personal loan to fund a deposit towards a BTL. See HMRC's Business Income manual at BIM45685 (tinyurl.com/2w75h9j8). Also, see HMRC's Property Income manual at PIM2052 (tinyurl.com/6mbsukaf), where it states: "Similarly, interest payable…on an overdraft is deductible where the asset is used for business purposes."

82. When Can A Re-Mortgage Be Tax Deductible?

Question: I am planning on re-mortgaging my residential property on a let-to-buy (BTL) mortgage, which means I will be moving out and renting my residential property and using the funds released to purchase another property for me to live in. The question is: will the interest on the let-to-buy be tax-deductible or not? I bought the property 14 years ago for £190,000 with a mortgage of £150,000. I have a balance left on the mortgage of £7,000, and the remortgage value is £300,000. Will the interest on the £300,000 be tax-deductible (or any portion of it)? If not, in what scenario would a remortgage be tax-deductible if I used the money to purchase BTL properties?

Answer: If you are getting a new mortgage of £300,000, your property must now be worth somewhat more than £300,000. If so, all the interest on the £300,000 loan will be tax-deductible (as per the 'section 24' rules introduced in April 2017) against your rental income, even though you are using the borrowed money to buy another property for you to live in. See HMRC's Business Income manual (BIM45700 at Example 2). This is because the borrowed money is less than the value of the property when you introduce the property into your property business (i.e. when you start to rent it out). If you used the borrowed money to purchase BTL properties, then even if the borrowed money was more than the value of the property when it started to be rented out, all the interest would be tax-deductible.

83. Buying And Transferring House To Son

Question: Our son is hoping to go to university in September. Rather than pay rent for four or five years, we thought it sensible to buy a property that he can live in and sublet one or two rooms to fellow students. He will be able to raise a deposit but the bank has said he can't get a buy-to-let mortgage in his own name as he will have no income (they won't count rental income); so we would, effectively, have to buy it for him and gift it to him when he starts working. What is the best way to minimise the tax he would have to pay when the property is transferred to him?

Answer: I appreciate that you are restricted by the rules imposed by the bank, but it would be best if your son could buy the property directly from the seller. Perhaps try convincing the bank that you will act as a guarantor for your son's mortgage? It may mean shopping around for the best mortgage deal. If that doesn't work, see if you can fit into the scenario described in the example in HMRC's Stamp Duty Land Tax manual at SDLTM09785 (tinyurl.com/xe38ke6j).

84. **Can I Claim Interest On The Additional Equity Property?**

    Question: I had extremely high equity in my first home, enough to split it up, leave 1/4 behind, and use 3/4 to buy a new family home. That original property was then mortgaged as a buy-to-let (BTL), and I claim the tax relief on the BTL mortgage interest as usual. I have read on several investors' blogs that the 1/4 that I did not carry into my new home can also be claimed as a cost of personal finance for the BTL. For example, BTL: valued at £160,000 – mortgage agreed for £120,000 @ 4%; home: valued at £200,000 – mortgage for £80.000 @2%. Instead, I could have put that £40,000 BTL equity into my own home and had lower interest. Can I claim 2% of the £40,000 interest? I assume I should claim for the reducing balance, as I am, of course, repaying capital on that £40,000. The balance reduces at approximately 3% per year.

    Answer: I am sorry, but I do not understand why you should be able to claim interest relief (of course, according to the new rules from April 2017 onwards) for interest that you could potentially have been paying but are not actually paying. In my experience, there is no such thing. Either the taxpayer has the responsibility or liability to pay the interest, or they do not.

85. **Nominating My New Purchase**

    Question: My wife and I are in the process of buying a second home in Brighton. I own the primary home, and she lives here too. Could I nominate the new purchase as a primary home to avoid stamp duty land tax (SDLT) and then change the nomination back to my present house? At that point, would I have to pay outstanding SDLT on the new second home? Or does HMRC let you off it? Our solicitor says we must pay the duty.

    Answer: You are referring to the additional 3% SDLT when one buys a second residential dwelling, and the exemption that applies when one buys a new main residence. However, the exemption that applies when purchasing a new main residence only applies when one disposes of the old main residence. See HMRC's Stamp Duty Land Tax manual (https://tinyurl.com/5u94urps). In your scenario, there has been no disposal; so your solicitor is correct.

86. **Can A Company Gift Money From The Sale Of A Property?**

    Question: My mother is the sole 100% shareholder and sole director of a limited company that owns a property. She would like to sell this property from the company to me for under market value. For example, the property is valued at £425,000 and I would be purchasing this for £300,000. My lender is happy with this based on me putting down 15% deposit based on the full market value which is £63,750 and the mortgage covers the remaining to make up it up to £300,000. The lender says the difference (i.e. £125,000) would be considered a gift. Are there any restrictions or laws to say that a limited company cannot gift the difference to myself as we are purchasing under market value?

    Answer: If you look at HMRC's Employment Income manual at EIM21601 (www.gov.uk/hmrc-internal-manuals/employment-income-manual/eim21601) and EIM21640 onwards ('Assets transferred to a director or employee at an undervalue'), you will see that there would be a tax charge on your mother for this £125,000. Even though the property is being transferred to you, and not your mother, your mother is the one who will be taxed. Also see EIM20504 (www.gov.uk/hmrc-internal-manuals/employment-income-manual/eim20504).

87. ### Change To Gas Central Heating: Revenue Or Capital?

   Question: Can I claim installing gas central heating, as well as supplying gas to my rented flat, as a revenue expense or is it a capital expense? The new system has five radiators which have replaced four old electric storage heaters and an electric fan heater in the bathroom.

   Answer: If you take a look at the end of HMRC's Property Income manual at PIM2020, it states: 'Even if the repairs are substantial...'. It seems to me that replacing a simple electric heater system with a full gas central heating system is an upgrade or improvement and not just a 'like for like replacement'. Therefore, it should be classified as a capital expense and not a revenue expense.

88. ### Company Or Privately Owned?

   Question: I am an overseas investor, planning to live in the UK in the future and becoming a full-time investor. Should I invest in buy-to-let (BTL) properties under my own name, or a company for a better tax position and transfer to my spouse in the future?

   Answer: This is not the forum to answer your question properly. But on a very basic level, it is generally better to invest personally. However, if this will result in you and your wife being higher rate taxpayers, and if you need to borrow to fund your investments so that 'section 24' restriction in tax relief for interest relief etc. rules become relevant, then you should consider a property investment company.

89. ### Tax Relief For Replacing Like-For-Like Sheds?

   Question: As a landlord, I am replacing the garden shed (which has now rotted) with one of the same. Can I claim tax relief for this?

   Answer: Please look at HMRC's Business Income manual at BIM35435, BIM35440, BIM35460 and subsequent pages on BIM35400. It seems to me that the whole shed is being replaced in its entirety and, therefore, this is capital expenditure and not revenue expenditure. Note there, the case of 'if an entire derelict wing of a large house were demolished and rebuilt.' However, I appreciate that this is not so clear cut and somewhat borderline.

90. ### Can Transferring A Property Maximise Our Personal Allowances?

   Question: I want to rent out a property on Airbnb. Will we pay less tax on income if we transfer it from joint ownership to my wife's name, as I pay high band tax and her pay is around £20,000 per annum?

   Answer: You are correct; if you transfer this property to your wife's ownership, instead of the rental income being received 50:50, it will be received 100% by your wife, and so there will be less income tax to pay.

91. Are Storage Costs An Allowable Expense?

Question: I am a private landlord, renting my flat out while I'm working away for a few years. I do not want to let the flat out fully furnished due to the extra complications that brings. Am I able to deduct the costs of storage from my tax liabilities?

Answer: Probably HMRC would argue that this is a private expense and not a business expense. If you would be renting out a furnished property and the furnishings would be used in the property business, and then a new tenant started who only wanted an unfurnished property, so you had to put all the furnishings into storage until this tenant stopped, you could probably claim storage costs. But in your scenario, the private furnishings have nothing to do with your property business.

92. Changing Th Rental Income Split

Question: I am in an unmarried relationship with my partner, and we have a property owned 50:50 that we rent out. I am a higher rate taxpayer and my partner is a basic rate taxpayer. Can we change the income so that my partner receives 90% of the rental income and thereby reduce my tax burden? If we can, how do we formalise this? Or do we need to formalise? Also, would it be possible for me to cover 90% of the costs and, therefore, improve my tax situation?

Answer: You can change the income so that your partner receives 90% of the rental income, and you receive 10% of the rental income (see HMRC's Property Income manual at PIM1030), as you have written. You should have a written agreement to this effect, and 90% of the rental income should go to your partner's personal bank account, and 10% to your personal bank account (see HMRC's Trusts, Settlements and Estates manual at TSEM9310). There isn't anything explicit I know of to answer your last question, but it seems to me that HMRC would expect that the person who receives 90% of the income should cover 90% of the costs.

93. Can My Daughter Live Rent Free?

Question: I have received a letter from HMRC stating that I may owe tax on rental income. The buy-to-let was originally set up on a private tenant but when they left the property, we moved our daughter in. She lives here rent-free but pays me £100 per month to cover insurance. We never got round to changing the buy-to-let mortgage but aimed to once the term was complete. What are the tax implications?

Answer: In actuality, the £100 per month you receive from your daughter is considered to be rent. However, if the £100 per month is truly equal to the amount you have to pay for insurance, then you have not made any profit on this rental because insurance is an allowable expense. I would recommend that you write to HMRC explaining that the £100 per month rent you receive is matched by your allowable expenses.

94. Non 50:50 Rental Income Split?

Question: I own a rental property with my parent in 50:50 shares as tenants-in-common. When I return to work after a maternity break, I will be a higher-rate taxpayer. My parent is a basic-rate taxpayer. Can we allocate the rental income differently (e.g., 25/75), so that my parent can be taxed on more rental income in their basic rate band than me? Do we have to change the beneficial ownership of the property to 25/75 and do a declaration of trust and Form 17? My income might change from year to year because I am a contractor. Can we change the allocation of rental income year by year?

Answer: Even though a property is owned 50:50 between A and B, they can agree to split the rental income in a different proportion. You do not need to change the beneficial ownership; you do not need to do any declaration of trust, and Form 17 is certainly not applicable. Preferably, you should have a written agreement between you. If A is to receive 25% and B is to receive 75%, then 25% of the rental income should go to A's personal bank account and 75% to B's personal bank account. It is possible to change the agreement year by year.

95. When Is Rental Income Taxable?

Question: I have received a letter from HMRC saying I may owe rental income. I have a buy-to-let (BTL) mortgage on a property I let my daughter live in rent-free; she pays me £100 per month to cover insurance. The BTL was originally set up on a private tenant, but they left the property and we moved our daughter in. We never got round to changing the BTL mortgage but aimed to once the term was complete. What are the tax implications?

Answer: Even though the £100 per month received from your daughter is to cover the insurances, it is still rental income (see HMRC's Property Income Manual at PIM1051). However, if it just covers the insurances, you have made no profit from this rental business, so there is no income tax liability. Assuming you have no other rental income, you do not need to declare this rental income, because you are making no profit, and it is below the £2,500/£10,000 HMRC reporting thresholds.

96. Will I Be Prosecuted For Forgetting To Declare Rental Income?

Question: I left my property and moved back in with my parents. I rented out the property through a property management company and I pay them a fee. I have used the rent to pay the mortgage. I am going to sell the property now but have just realised that I should have been paying income tax on the rent received. This is not a business. I work full-time and pay my tax and National Insurance contributions. What should I do? I don't want to be prosecuted.

Answer: HMRC's publication on making a disclosure under its 'Let Property Campaign' (www.gov.uk/government/publications/let-property-campaign-your-guide-to-making-a-disclosure/let-property-campaign-your-guide-to-making-a-disclosure) includes guidance for taxpayers approaching HMRC of their own accord to disclose that they have failed to declare rental income. You won't be prosecuted. But it is much better if you come to HMRC first, than rather than vice versa.

97. What Expenses Can I Claim On Tax Return?

Question: We own a property which was let out to a tenant for about seven or eight years. When she moved into the property, it was immaculate but when she moved out, it was a wreck. We had to do a full refurbishment, including a new kitchen, new double glazing, flooring, new internal doors, new radiators and redecoration throughout. Am I able to claim this back on my tax return?

Answer: A repair restores the property to its original position and so is classed as revenue expenditure, which can be offset against rental income. By contrast, an improvement adds something to the property that was not there before and is therefore generally classed as capital expenditure, which can only be offset against a capital gain when the property is eventually sold. So, if the new kitchen is essentially a like-for-like replacement, it can be treated as revenue expenditure. Decorating is usually revenue expenditure. HMRC accepts that replacing single glazing with double glazing is revenue expenditure, since double glazing has become the 'industry standard' nowadays. The like-for-like rule would similarly apply to the new flooring, doors and radiators. See HMRC's Property Income Manual at PIM2025 and PIM2030.

98. Can Costs of Condemned Boiler Be Deducted?

Question: I have had to replace the boiler in a house that I am selling, as the old one was condemned. The replacement is like-for-like. Can I offset the cost for capital gains tax (CGT) purposes?

Answer: Since the replacement boiler was a like-for-like replacement it is not an improvement, so not an allowable expense for CGT purposes. But the cost could be offset against rental income if this is a rental property. See HMRC's Capital Gains Manual at CG10260, where it states: "Similarly, any expenditure which is or in some circumstances might be allowable in the computation of an income tax liability or notional liability is not allowable expenditure for Capital Gains Tax purposes." See also HMRC's Property Income Manual at PIM2030.

Capital Gains Tax

99. Any Tax If I Sell My Home?

Question: I have a property which I lived in for three years and then let out for one year. I am now going to sell the property. Will I be liable to pay any tax?

Answer: No. You will not be liable to pay any capital gains tax. This is because the last 18 months of ownership are exempt from tax, and so is the period that the property was your main residence. This means that the first three years of ownership are covered by private residence relief and the last year of ownership is covered by the last 18 month of ownership rule.

Therefore, no tax is due.

100. How Can We Transfer The Property?

Question: My husband and I bought a house specifically for our daughter to live in 12 years ago because she was expecting a baby. We paid a deposit of £50,000 and have a mortgage for the balance of £150,000. Our daughter paid all the monthly mortgage amounts and has spent approximately £50,000 on a loft extension and renovations. We are about to retire and would like our deposit back from her and transfer the house into her name. How can we prove that she has the beneficial interest to HMRC, such that if we transfer it into her name we do not pay a huge amount of capital gains tax?. There is still £80,000 outstanding on the mortgage (eight years remaining) but we could possibly borrow this to redeem it on the understanding she would re-mortgage the house, once it was in her name, and repay us. The house is currently worth approximately £450,000.

Answer: If you look at HMRC's guidance in the Capital Gains manual (at www.gov.uk/hmrc-internal-manuals/capital-gains-manual/cg70230, second bullet point) you can see that you may have an argument to say that the house has always been beneficially owned by your daughter, even though it was not originally put into writing. Furthermore, if you look at CG65406 you can see that if you put things into writing now it would help (although there are other contrary indications on the HMRC manuals). If so, merely transferring the legal ownership now to your daughter will not involve any CGT (see CG10720).

101. Can I Select Any Property As My PPR?

Question: I currently live with my parents and have purchased two investment properties that are currently rented out. Am I able to nominate one of the let properties as my principle private residence to benefit from the PPR relief?

Answer: PPR is only available to the owner of a house if he occupied it as his only or main residence. An intention to occupy it is not sufficient.

It is not necessary to have lived in it as the only or main residence for all the period of ownership, but for at least part of the period of ownership it must have been the only or main residence.

The HMRC say in IR Interpretation 73 that 'it is the quality of occupation rather than the length of occupation which determines whether a dwelling-house is its owner's residence'.

102. Can I Offset Costs If I Have Lived In The Property?

Question: When the first part of property ownership is claimed as residential ownership (i.e. I live in the property) can:

- purchase costs of the property be claimed as relief
- refurbishment costs, carried out during the residential period, be claimed as relief

... when I decide to sell the property?

Answer: The simple answer to this question is yes - both purchase costs and major refurbishment costs can be added to the acquisition costs of the property, to set off against the sale proceeds, to reduce the capital gain when the property is disposed of.

Case Study:

> Louise buys her first home in August 1998 for £50,000. The purchasing costs are £700 and include solicitor's fees, survey fees etc.
>
> In May 1991, she has a conservatory built. The cost of this is £15,000.
>
> In June 1995, she moves in with her long-term boyfriend and rents her property out.
>
> She finally decides to sell her first home in June 2014, she is able to claim relief on the £700 purchasing costs and the cost of the conservatory against the capital gain.

103. Can I Sell My Property Below Market Value?

Question: My house (my only property) is perhaps valued at £190,000. Can I sell it to my daughter (a single parent) for less than this?

Answer: You can sell your house to your daughter for whatever figure you want. However, for tax purposes it is deemed that you sold it to her for its present market value – the figure it would fetch on the open market in an arm's length sale to a third party. For tax purposes this is the figure for which you are deemed to sell it, and it is also the figure your daughter is deemed to buy it for. In your case, it would appear to be £190,000. If this house is your principal private residence, then the sale should not trigger any capital gains tax liability for you. This can be seen on page www.hmrc.gov.uk/manuals/cgmanual/CG14530.htm of the HMRC Capital Gains Manual.

104. When Should We Gift Our Son a Property We Are Buying?

Question: We are currently looking to buy a property for cash which we will then rent out. We would like this to be for our son who will soon be 17. Is there any way we can do this at the time of purchase?

Answer: Since your son is under 18 he cannot legally own property. So, you can purchase the property in your names as the legal owners (bare trustees or nominees), so that your names will be on the official documents, and instruct the solicitor to draw up a deed of trust at the time of purchase explaining that your son has the beneficial ownership of the property. When he becomes 18 it is a simple procedure to transfer the legal ownership to him.

105. Tax Implications, If Any, Of Selling Part Of My Garden?

Question: I am currently discussing selling part of the garden of our only residential property and would like to know if tax is payable on the proceeds. The land would probably be sold to a builder for the construction of two semi-detached houses.

Answer: The capital gains tax exemption for principal private residence includes grounds not exceeding half a hectare (approximately 1 1/4 acres), or such larger area as is appropriate to the size and character of the house. If some of the land is sold, including for the purpose of building plots, the sale is covered by the exemption so long as the land was enjoyed as part of the garden and grounds, and is sold before the house is sold or at the same time the house is sold (but not after the house is sold).

106. Do I Have To Live In It To Be Exempt From Tax?

Question: If I bought a plot of land and built a house, would I pay tax if I sold it and used all the sale proceeds to purchase another property or land, or would I have to live in it firstly as my principal private residence (PPR)? If I move in, how long do I have to live there for exemption?

Answer: If you sell the house without living in it - yes, you will be liable to tax. If you live in it before you sell it - you can make it into your PPR. There is no fixed answer to how long you need to live in it to make it your PPR. You need to be able to demonstrate that you moved in with the intention to stay long term. Some tax advisers would say you need to live in it for at least between six months and a year.

107. Do I Have More Than One PPR?

Question: I am aged 78 and a retired builder with a property with a garden, in total under 0.5 hectares. I lived in this house for 5 years around 11 years ago, and whilst living in it got planning permission to build two houses in the garden. I sold off the two plots for £120,000 and £150,000 respectively and kept the house as a holiday home. With the proceeds of the two plots sold I then bought another property which I have lived in for the past 6 years. I want to go back to living in the house which is now the holiday home and sell the one I am in now. Please can you tell me my PPR position?

Answer: See www.hmrc.gov.uk/manuals/cgmanual/CG64545.htm where it is explained that, when the taxpayer does not make an election, his PPR is a matter of fact - i.e. where he lived as his main home determines which of his two houses is his PPR. So, for the first 5 years the original house (A) was your PPR, and then when you moved into the new house (B), B became your PPR for those 6 years. If you now move back to A, A will become your PPR again and B will stop being your PPR. A taxpayer cannot have two PPRs concurrently, except for the last 36-month rule, which allows a taxpayer to claim PPR relief for the last 36 months' ownership of a property, even though he is living in a different property as his PPR during those 36 months.

As from April 2014 the last 36-month rule has been shortened to 18 months.

108. How Long In A Property Before I Get PPR?

Question: What is the minimum amount of time you need to live in a property before you can claim 'Private Residence Relief'? I have heard it is 6 months, is this true?

Answer: The HMRC has not given any specific guidance as to how long you need to live in a property before you can claim the relief. However, as a general rule of thumb, you should look to make it your **permanent residence** for at least 1 year, i.e. 12 months (but it can be less and there have been successful cases for much less than this). The longer you live in a property the better chance you have of claiming the relief. The HMRC is not necessarily interested in how long you lived in the property. They are more interested in whether the property really was your home!

If you want to claim this relief, then here are some pointers that will help you to convince the taxman that a property genuinely was your private residence.

- Have utility bills in your own name at the property address.
- Make the property address your voting address on the electoral register.
- Be able to demonstrate that you bought furniture and furnishings for the property. Keep receipts and prove that bulky furniture was delivered to the property address under your name.
- Have all bank statements delivered to the property address.

109. Can I Defer Capital Gains Tax?

Question: I am about to sell a buy-to-let property that has made a £40,000 gain. But I am looking to re-invest this money back into another two more properties. Because I have re-invested the money can I defer paying any tax that is due on the £40,000 profit?

Answer: This is a very commonly asked question and one which is often misunderstood by too many people. Once you have disposed of the buy-to-let property then you are liable to pay capital gains tax. This is regardless of whether you have re-invested the profits or spent the money.

There are only two exceptions to this. One is 'Furnished Holiday Lets'. The other is if the property is the subject of compulsory purchase (or compulsory acquisition by a lessee).

110. What CGT Liability For Property That Is Partly PPR?

Question: Please could you tell me what capital gains tax (CGT) each party would pay if there was a 50/50 ownership at sale, but it was one of the owner's primary residence?

Answer: If A and B own a property 50:50, then the sale proceeds and the base cost of the property are divided in two, and two separate CGT calculations are made, one for A and one for B. If it is A's principle private residence, then A will be exempt from any CGT, but B will be liable in the normal way on B's half. This kind of scenario can occur in a divorce situation, when A stays in the property, and B moves out.

Sometime later the property is sold, but since moving out it is no longer B's PPR. The last eighteen months of ownership of B will be deemed to be occupied and therefore eligible for PPR relief, because previously B actually occupied the property.

111. Can I Increase Borrowing To Minimise Or Avoid CGT?

Question: I have a house for sale for £115,000. At present I owe £75,000 on it. If I increase the borrowing on it tomorrow to £105,000, then sell it for £115,000 in 8 weeks' time, will I have to pay tax on the £10,000 profit? I do not live in the property.

Answer: The CGT liability is based on the purchase and selling price of the property not on the amount that is owed on the property. For CGT purposes, it does not matter what the outstanding finance is on the property. Therefore, if you purchased your property for £50,000 and sold it for £115,000 then you could be liable to pay tax at 18% or 28% on the £65,000 profit. This is even if you owe £115,000 on the property.

112. Do I Pay CGT If I Build Apartments In My Residence?

Question: I am planning to extend my property (principle private residence) to build two apartments. While I would continue to live in my current property, I want to sell the two new apartments. Do I have to pay any tax from the gains? If yes, then how can it be reduced?

Answer: If the new apartments are essentially separate from the original dwelling with their own entrances, for tax purposes they will be considered separately. Therefore, they will not benefit from principal private residence relief except on the land on which they are built. This assumes that the land was used until now for the enjoyment of the taxpayers dwelling.

So, tax will have to be paid on the profit on the apartments.

From your message, it seems as though you are doing this as a property development project, not with the intention of keeping long term. If so, the profit will be subject to income tax like any trading income.

If you are a basic rate taxpayer and can take dividends from a limited company, it may be worth exploring the possibility of doing the project through a limited company.

113. Will I Be Able To Avoid CGT By Helping My Brother?

Question: I purchased a house for my bankrupt and penniless Brother-in-law in June 2003. He was then 78 years old and is now 80 years old. I have paid all the bills relating to this house except the bills from the utilities. When he dies, am I exempt Capital Gains Tax on this property, assuming the property has increased in value?

Answer: Unfortunately, you are not exempt from Capital Gains Tax (CGT) when he dies.
If you would have put the property into trust when you purchased it and then let your Brother-in-law occupy it, you could have avoided any CGT when he died.

This shows the importance of advanced tax planning!

It may be worth your while speaking to a tax consultant to see whether the application of the 'implied trust rules' are relevant to your situation. In short, the 'implied trust rules' are based on a situation in which person A owns a property and person B lives in it. However, in very special circumstances person A can get PPR despite there not being a trust in place.

As mentioned, this only applies to very special circumstances and professional advice needs to be sought.

114. Is There CGT Due On A Property Purchased For My Mother?

Question: I purchased a house in 1984 for the sole purpose of my mother to live there rent free. I paid the mortgage and all maintenance bills. My mother paid the utility bills. My mother has now passed away and I intend to sell the house. Am I liable for capital gains tax?

Answer: A property owned on 5 April 1988, that has been continuously occupied rent free by a dependent relative since that date, is exempt from capital gains tax (CGT) when disposed of, by virtue of Taxation of Chargeable Gains Act (TCGA) 1992 section 226. A dependent relative includes a mother who has no husband, and also usually includes a mother over 65.

115. Can I Buy Property For A Child Under The Age Of 18?

Question: We are considering buying a property which will be let. Is there a way to buy this property for a child who is 13? Is it possible to put it in some form of trust for your child in order to decrease the tax burden? For example, CGT tax, etc.

Answer: A minor under the age of 18 cannot own land or property in the UK, so it would have to be owned in trust by trustees, e.g. parents, for the beneficial ownership of the 13-year-old. Any asset owned by a child under 18 and unmarried, derived from the property of the parents that produces income of more than £100 per year, is taxed on the parents as the parent's income.

However, this doesn't apply for CGT purposes.

One possible solution is to create a 'bare' trust. A 'Bare' trust can be created where the child is the beneficial owner, and the parents are the legal owners who hold the property effectively as nominees. When the property is sold, it will be taxed only on the child (who will have their own CGT annual exemption and perhaps lower tax bands - if they don't have much other income) and not on the parents.

But it must be remembered that the child cannot be prevented from having the property put into his own legal ownership at age 18.

116. Can I Use Remainder Of My CGT Allowance?

Question: I sold a property and used up £3,000 of my annual CGT allowance as there was only a £3,000 profit. Will I now lose the remaining allowance?

Answer: No, you will not lose the remaining part of the allowance as long as it is used within the remainder of the tax year. The Annual CGT allowance must be used within the tax year. There is no need to use it all in one go, but an unused amount cannot be carried forward into the following tax year.

117. Can I Claim Unused CGT For Previous Years?

Question: I understand that there is a capital gains tax allowance, but I was told that you can claim an allowance for previous years. Is this so, and how does it work?

Answer: You have been misinformed. It is not possible to claim capital gains tax allowances for previous years. You are only able to use the CGT allowance of the current year. If you fail to make use of it and the tax year changes then you can only use the allowance in the current year.

118. Can I Transfer My CGT Allowance?

Question: My partner has a property in his sole name. Can I transfer my unused CGT allowance to him so he can utilise my allowance as well?

Answer: No this is not possible. Only the people owning the property can use their CGT allowances.

119. How Can My Partner Reduce CGT?

Question: My Partner and I live together in my house. We are not married and he does not pay any mortgage or bills here. He bought a house close by that he rents out and has never lived in. We now wish to sell his house and for him to move in here on a more permanent basis.

Is it possible for him to move into his house for the time being to limit capital gains tax as he has never lived there, there is no PPR as it stands, he lived away. I had had a very nasty divorce I was not willing for him to be put on this mortgage and advised him to keep a foot on the housing ladder.

Now it seems he is liable for CGT if he sells. Any advice on this would be great!

Answer: This is a frequently asked question. The answer is unfortunately not clear cut. However, it may be fair to say that; a) if your partner has no other property that is eligible to be his PPR because he owns no other residence, nor does he rent any other residence, and; b) he moves into this (until now) investment property with all his belongings 'lock, stock and barrel' and informs every one of his new address, and; c) he stays there and lives there fully for six months to a year, then more than likely the HMRC would accept that this residence is his PPR.

Concerning point, a, even if he has another property that is eligible to be his PPR, if he makes an election to the HMRC that the residence that he is moving into now is now his PPR and not the other residence, then it will legitimately become his PPR.

120. What Is The Tax Date For CGT Purposes?

Question: What is the tax date for CGT purposes? Is it the date the contracts are exchanged or the date the completion takes place.

Answer: There is a common misconception that the tax date for a sale of a property is the completion date of a property. This is not true. The tax date for CGT purposes is actually the date the contracts are exchanged.

121. How Do I Work Out Capital Gains Tax (CGT)?

Question: I have two houses, both on buy to let mortgages, and I am thinking of selling one house; can you please tell me about CGT and how is it best to work this out because I have a mortgage on the house.

Answer: CGT is calculated on the difference between the sale proceeds and the acquisition value / price, i.e. how much you get for selling it and how much you paid for it. The fact that you have a mortgage, or how much the mortgage is, is not relevant to CGT in normal circumstances (this is a mistake that many people make - you are in good company!).

The mortgage is relevant to CGT only in a scenario in which the purchaser takes over the mortgage from the seller, as part of the deal. In such circumstances, tax law adds the amount of the mortgage taken over to the amount actually paid by the seller to determine the final selling price. See www.gov.uk/hmrc-internal-manuals/capital-gains-manual/cg12706 , on HMRC Capital Gains Manual.

122. If We Sell At A Loss, Will We Still Have To Pay CGT?

Question: We are looking to move and are considering a buy-to-let scheme on our house in order to rent this property out. We purchased the property at £250K and it is currently valued at £230K. If we rent the property out for a year or two and then sell at £230K, will we still have to pay CGT even though the sale was at loss to the original purchase price?

Answer: If you look on HMRC website Capital Gains Manual at page CG14200 (www.hmrc.gov.uk/manuals/cgmanual/cg14200.htm) you can see that the capital gains computation is simply the disposal proceeds less the original expenditure. In your case this results in a negative £20,000 figure so you will have no CGT to pay.

123. Is There A Capital Gains Risk And/or An Offset?

Question: Twenty years ago, I inherited a house and some land. I ran cattle on the land as a small-holding until 15 years ago. A neighbour has offered a considerable amount for 1 acre adjacent to their house. I am self-employed earning around £20,000 a year. How do I sit with capital gains tax (CGT) and any potential to offset the gain by buying other land?

Answer: If you would be selling the land at the same time as stopping your business, then maybe entrepreneur's relief would be available to reduce the CGT, due to the 'associated disposal' rules. However, since the gap between the two in this case is 15 years, this relief cannot apply - see www.hmrc.gov.uk/manuals/cgmanual/CG64000.htm at the end of *Example 2*. Rolling over the gain by investing in some other land is also not an option in your circumstance - it has been too long since you ceased trading, and rollover relief is not available for investment property.

124. Will This Avoid CGT?

Question: If my husband and I both I gift our daughter part of our buy-to-let (BTL) house each year (and the gift is under our annual CGT allowance) can my husband and I still take all the rental income? We want her to eventually own the BTL house but we're trying to avoid paying CGT on the gift.

Answer: You can draw up a written agreement (preferably before the start of the tax year) that even though the house is owned 90:10 or 80:20 etc., nevertheless the rental income is going all to you and your husband. Thereafter make sure the rental income actually goes to the bank account of you and your husband (I assume your daughter is over 18).

125. Should I Move Into Previously Rented Out Property?

Question: If I buy a 2nd property and rent it out for a couple of years, is any tax due on it if I then sell my primary residence and move into this 2nd property making it my primary residence for the next 10 years before selling it?

Answer: If you sell your first (primary residence) property and if it has been classed as your main residence then there will be no tax due on this property. If after two years you then move into the previous rented property, then you may well have a small CGT liability in the future.

However, a huge chunk of the tax liability will be avoided because you will benefit from private residence relief. However, you will also receive another favourable tax relief i.e. private letting relief.

The latter relief along with your annual CGT allowance could well wipe-out any CGT liability. However, in the case that a CGT liability still remains, it is likely to be nominal when compared with the gain you have made on the property.

126. Can I Give A Family Member A Financial Gift?

Question: Can I give a family member a financial gift and account for it within my self-assessment returns?

Answer: You can certainly give a family member a financial gift. However, you do not account for it on a self-assessment return, unless it is an asset that would be assessable to capital gains tax (CGT) had you disposed of it to a third party.

As far as income tax is concerned, it has no impact. This is because I assume it is a pure gift, and not in return for any work performed.

As far as Inheritance Tax (IHT) is concerned, it is a Potentially Exempt Transfer (PET), and falls out of any IHT calculations if the donor survives for seven years. The HMRC do not need to be informed of PET's during lifetime.

As far as CGT is concerned, if it is a non-cash asset that is worth more at the time of disposal than at the time of acquisition, then it is quite possible that the donor is liable to CGT on the gift, even though he/she receives nothing from the recipient in return for the property.

127. How Do You 'Gift A Property In Stages'?

Question: How do you 'gift a property in stages' to use annual CGT exemptions?

Answer: Gifting a property in stages is the same as gifting a whole property. Your solicitor will draw up the required documents for the conveyance of a percentage of the property and register the transaction with the Land Registry.

In order to calculate what percentage to transfer, you need to look at the present market value of the property, its acquisition cost, any principal private residence and letting relief available, and choose a percentage that reduces the gain to approximately the annual exemption available.

128. Avoiding Tax When Splitting A Property

Question: My mother and I have lived in our house for 35 years. I have converted the house into 2 dwellings and intend to have separate leases on them. Will we be liable for CGT at any time? If so, what is the best way to avoid this?

Answer: This question is not very clear so I need to make some assumptions. I assume that the mother owned the whole house until they decided to split the house in two, at which point she transferred ownership of half of it to the child. If so, there will be no capital gains tax liability because principal private residence relief will be available on both halves of the house.

The mother owned the whole house until the split and lived in it. She owned and lived in her half after the split. The child owned and lived in their half after the split. So, the conditions for the relief have been complied with and there will be no tax due.

129. Tax Treatment For New And Replacement Kitchens

Question: We recently bought a property for Buy-to-let. It needed a new kitchen before it could be let. We also had to redecorate throughout. Obviously, we will have to redecorate again between each tenancy.

Is the cost of original decoration offset against rental income or CGT when we sell? Also, what if we have to put in another new kitchen before reselling? Can we claim the cost of 2 new kitchens against CGT?

Answer: In short, the first kitchen replacement would appear to be a capital expense and any subsequent kitchen replacements a revenue expense (i.e. can be offset against the rental income). See www.gov.uk/hmrc-internal-manuals/property-income-manual/pim2020.

According to the HMRC guidelines, I believe that the first new kitchen is a capital expense because the property was unable to be let out until the kitchen was replaced. Also, a new kitchen is likely to have increased the value of a property.

However, the subsequent replacement kitchens are just re-instating a worn out or dilapidated asset and are therefore a revenue expense. The redecorating is a revenue expense as the HMRC states that:

Examples of common repairs, which are normally deductible in computing rental business profits, include:

- exterior and interior painting and decorating;
- stone cleaning;
- damp and rot treatment;
- mending broken windows, doors, furniture and machines such as cookers or lifts;
- re-pointing; and
- replacing roof slates, flashing and gutters.

It would seem to me that a property can usually be let out even though it needs redecorating and therefore any costs incurred for re-decorating prior to and during lets can be offset against the rental income.

130. What Tax If I Immediately Sell An Inherited Property?

Question: I am a house owner and am about to inherit a 2nd property (worth approx. 150k) which solicitors (executors of the will) are about to put in my name.

If I sell it straight away would I avoid Capital Gains Tax (presumably yes as I will not make more than 11K from the time I get it and actually sell it). My main concern is, as it will be my 2nd property, would I have to pay more/extra CGT or be a victim of another tax/charge?

Answer: When someone dies, and passes an asset to an inheritor, the inheritor receives the asset, for tax purposes, at probate value, i.e. market value at the time of death. There is no capital gains tax on death, but there is an uplift, i.e. the recipient receives it at present market value.

131. How Is Property Ownership Determined?

Question: My 2 brothers-in-law live in the same house and are joint owners. One of them is getting married and is moving out. When he moves out, will he still retain ownership of his share of the property?

He has suggested that his brother buy him out and is willing to accept about 50% of the value of his share of the property, which is approx. £100k. Are there any tax implications to this move? The property is worth approx. £200k.

Answer: When the brother moves out he will still retain ownership of his share of the property. If the present market value of the property is £200K and he sells 50% of the property (i.e. his share) to his brother (i.e. a connected person) then the HMRC will treat this as a sale for £100K, whether he actually receives £100K from his brother or not.

This figure of £100K is what he will have to use in his capital gains tax (CGT) computation.

If he has lived in the property all the period of ownership, the disposal is exempt from CGT due to principal private residence relief.

132. Can My Brother Discount His Share Of Property?

Question: My brother and I bought a property jointly but the deeds are registered solely in his name. Neither of us have used the property as a main residence. The property was rented over the period and all rents were declared. The purchase price for this property was £50,000 and the current market value is £150,000.

Can my brother now sell this property to me below the market value (e.g. £100,000) to reduce the CGT on the sale?

Answer: It is not clear to me whether you have always had beneficial ownership over half the property, since the date of acquisition, or not i.e. did the contribution of half the purchase price make you an owner of half the beneficial ownership of the house, even though your brother was the legal owner, or was the contribution of half the purchase price by you simply a loan by you to your brother?

An important factor in deciding this question is in whose name was the rental income declared to the Revenue. If it was declared only in your brother's name, this shows that your brother had beneficial ownership over the whole property (see Revenue Capital Gains Manual page CG70230.)

133. What Tax Will I Pay On A Transferred Property?

Question: A close friend (non-relative) of mine will shortly be transferring three properties across to me at no cost; I will not pay anything for them. She owns the properties outright and there is no debt secured against them. There are personal reasons for this, which are perfectly legitimate i.e. this is not an attempt of falsifying bankruptcy etc. My intention is to rent out two of the properties and sell the third at its current market price of £230,000. Given that I have never lived in this property, I assume I will be liable for CGT. However, I am unsure how to calculate this especially given that I paid £0 for the property.

Answer: If you look at page CG14530 (www.hmrc.gov.uk/manuals/cgmanual/cg14530.htm) of HMRC's Capital Gains Manual, you will see that in certain situations 'market value' is substituted, for taxation purposes, for the consideration that changes hands. The amount that the recipient/purchaser of the asset actually pays the donor/seller is ignored.

134. What Is The Tax Position On Transfers?

Question: I bought some land with one house on it in 1987, and my parents lived in it. The land and house were transferred to my parents in 1991 with no capital gains tax (CGT). I built a house in the garden of the original house while still owned and occupied by my parents and the new house has been transferred back to me. Are there any tax liabilities for either my parents or me?

Answer: I am not sure what you mean by 'transferred back to you'. I would have presumed that if you built the house, obviously with your parents' consent, then the house was yours from 'day 1'. If so the only problem is the land underneath the house. If your parents transfer it to you, then it is quite likely that there is no CGT for them to pay, because most probably they used the land before the building began, and such a transfer is therefore eligible for principal private residence relief. If I am wrong, and the new house belonged to your parents from the beginning, then most probably they will be liable to income tax on its transfer to you.

135. Would I Have To Pay Capital Gains Tax?

Question: I brought my flat in July 2006 and lived there until April 2010 when I moved into my now wife's house. We rented out the flat due to the negative equity on the property. Now as the market has improved it is on the market. We are also buying my wife's parents' house jointly with my sister and brother in law, if I reinvest any profit from my sale into the purchase of my wife's parents house do I need to pay any capital gains tax?

Answer: Unfortunately, in this country there is no rollover/holdover/reinvestment relief for residential investment property except in two not so usual circumstances: (a) qualifying furnished holiday lettings; and (b) compulsory purchase. However, since you lived in the property from 2006 until 2010 and then rented it out, it is quite possible that you may not have much capital gains tax (CGT) to pay, due to a combination of principal private residence relief, lettings exemption and the CGT annual exemption.

136. Which Valuation Figure Would Be Used?

Question: I have lived in my home for 12 years and in that time added a whopping extension. I am hoping to build a new home and move into that, while keeping the second home and letting it. I realise there is an 18-month's extension, but my question is what happens after that? Say I paid £200,000 for my house, then spent a further £100,000 (eight years ago) on extending it. The valuation is therefore considerably more than it would be had we not extended, i.e. when we come to sell let's say the value is £600,000, but had we not extended, £450,000. How does this come into effect with capital gains tax (CGT)? As I understand it, we'd be taxed for CGT for the percentage of time we weren't in the property (plus 18 months), so surely that's unfair as the 'profit' (for want of a better word) was made while in occupation (by natural increases plus the extension). Is there any way I could get a valuation now (or in 18 months), and then pay the CGT on the difference (between sale price and valuation) when we come to sell?

Answer: The way it works for capital gains tax is that you take the entire gain (e.g. £600,000 less £200,000 less £100,000 = £300,000) and divide it by all the years of ownership. Let's say you move out today and sell in three years' time, so your years of ownership are 15. Your capital gain per year is £20,000. The first 12 years are exempt, as are the last 18 months of ownership. So, you are only taxable on the 18 months starting today, which equates to a capital gain of £30,000. If you let out the house during this 18-month period you are eligible for the letting exemption, to reduce the £30,000. Unfortunately, the rules do not agree with your suggested method of calculation.

137. Will There Be A Capital Gains Tax Liability?

Question: If we sell one rental property and, after paying off the mortgage, use the balance to repay the loan on another rental property (which we will keep for the moment) would that balance be liable for capital gains tax (CGT) since it is reinvesting in the same business?

Answer: Not just that balance, but the difference between the sale proceeds and what you paid for that property will all be liable to CGT. Even though you are reinvesting in the same business, unfortunately in this country there is no holdover/rollover or reinvestment relief for a capital gain on a residential investment property except for: (a) compulsory purchase; (b) furnished holiday lettings; or (c) under the enterprise investment scheme rules, which are not compatible with investment in residential property.

138. **Do I Pay Tax On What I Won't Receive?**

    Question: I'm from Spain, originally, and my parents own a house there. I live in the UK permanently now and am UK tax resident. After my mother's passing, I inherited one-sixth of the house, but that value was never transferred to me - the house was to remain my father's. He is now planning to sell the property to buy a smaller apartment. Will I need to pay tax on my share of the money, even though again - I will not receive it in anyway?

    Answer: Strictly speaking, yes. It seems to me that you inherited ownership of one-sixth of the house, but either your father had the right to live in it, or even if he didn't have the right, he did so anyway. Now that the house is being sold, if it is worth more than it was when your mother died, then you are making a capital gain. Being UK resident, you are liable to UK tax on your worldwide capital gains. If there is Spanish tax on this sale, most likely you will be eligible to double tax relief. As for not receiving any of the sale proceeds, I would imagine that you have a one-sixth share of the new apartment. Most likely this is an internal family matter that needs to be sorted out in a 'diplomatic' way.

139. **Can I Minimise Capital Gains Tax?**

    Question: I bought a property for my parents 20 years ago, and have since extended and improved it significantly. Obviously, no rent has been paid. I do not own another home. What is my position regarding minimising capital gains tax (CGT)?

    Answer: You will have to pay CGT when you sell the property, like any other property that is not your main residence. You can reduce the capital gain by the amount of your capital expenditure over the years (see www.gov.uk/hmrc-internal-manuals/property-income-manual/pim2020 for the definition of capital expenditure). There used to a relief for dependant relatives, but it is not relevant to you.

140. **Would We Be Liable For Capital Gains Tax?**

    Question: We have lived in our current property for ten years, and seven years ago, spent approximately £150,000 having a large extension doubling the property. Now our children have married and left home, we are looking at creating two properties from the one by separating the extension from the original property, allowing us to stay in our home but sell off the extension to pay off our mortgage. Would we be liable for capital gains tax, as the cost of the extension relates to the part we are trying to sell?

    Answer: It seems from what you have written that the extension became part of your home, and you lived in it as your main residence. If so when you sell it off, you will be eligible for principal private residence relief and there should be no capital gains tax. See www.gov.uk/hmrc-internal-manuals/capital-gains-manual/cg64236, CG64240 and CG64245.

141. Do I Need Receipts To Claim Against Capital Gains Tax?

Question: Sixteen years ago, I had to substantially renovate a buy-to-let property in order to make it habitable for letting purposes. If I sold the property now, would the taxman require receipts for the work done if I claim the amount against any capital gain?

Answer: Most likely the taxman will not ask you for receipts. However, you should have kept them (www.gov.uk/hmrc-internal-manuals/self-assessment-legal-framework/salf211). If you do claim this capital expenditure and the taxman does write to you asking for proof, you will have to explain that you didn't keep the receipts (if that is the case).

142. Can I Contest The Valuation?

Question: My brother and I were gifted a house by my mum and stepdad in January 2014. They bought the house in 2004 for approximately £195,000. The value on the land registry title absolute recorded at the time of transfer to me and my brother in 2014 was stated as being 'between £100,001 and £200,000. If my brother and I were to sell the property now for an approximate value of £300,000 how much CGT would we pay? Is it affected by the stated value at time of transfer in 2014? If so, is there any way I can contest this valuation, as it is definitely wrong. The house is in London and is almost certainly above the £200,000 valuation given in 2014 and definitely above the £100,000 valuation. The property has been rented out the entire time it has been owned by my parents or me and my brother.

Answer: You can certainly contest this valuation. A house in London bought for £195,000 in 2004 must have been (under normal circumstances) worth a lot more in 2014. You are not bound by what was written on the land registry documents. See www.gov.uk/hmrc-internal-manuals/capital-gains-manual/cg14530 and www.gov.uk/hmrc-internal-manuals/capital-gains-manual/cg16230.

143. How Can We Manage The Separation/Divorce Split?

Question: My wife suddenly walked out of the marriage in late February, not leaving time to transfer equity in the tax year. We are partners in two properties and she has one solely in her name and I have six. The joint ones are mortgaged; three of mine are fully paid and so is hers. The two joint owned properties are blocks of ten and twelve respectively. I am deeply worried that any settlement of our assets is going to cause a tax bill that was never planned for and fear it could wipe out the property business leaving both of us with a greatly reduced income. I have no problem with our separation and no divorce proceedings have been initiated by either of us. I have no issues with dividing the properties into equal shares but I do have issues with having to pay capital gains tax (CGT) that was never planned and so budgeted for. Two of the paid-for properties we lived in as our principal private residence for a number of years, and another for about a month, which is mortgaged. How could this situation be best managed so that CGT isn't an issue?

Answer: You are referring to the CGT rule that if a transfer is made between a husband and wife in a tax year in which they were living together for at least part of the year, then it is 'no gain, no loss', and no CGT is charged on the transfer. But if the transfer takes place in a year in which they are permanently separated, then it is deemed to take place at current market value, and if this is more than acquisition value there will be a CGT charge. See HMRC's Capital Gains manual at CG22500. If you wait to make any transfers between you until after the decree absolute, and the transfers are not made under a court order, the sale price agreed between you will be used for the CGT computation, unless it differs substantially from the expected market value, in which case market value will be substituted. See HMRC's guidance at CG22505. So, it seems that you cannot escape too much from current market value. If possible, maybe your wife would consider getting back together with you for a short time in the current tax year, for the sake of saving tax, so that the first sentence above would apply. If that is out of the question, the CGT relief explained in the Capital Gains manual at CG73000P ('Relief on exchange of joint interests in land') may possibly be applied to the two jointly owned properties. This would require professional tax advice.

144. Gifting Property Over Seven Years

Question: I am single and I currently own a number of buy-to-let properties in Yorkshire. The value of my assets is over £500,000, and one of the properties is valued at £240,000. Can I gift this property (debt-free) to my nephew over a seven-year-period, and what would the tax implications be to myself and my nephew?

Answer: You can gift this property over a seven-year period, presumably about 14% per year. You would need to calculate the capital gain on the whole house each year and take 14% of this figure. You would have a capital gains tax (CGT) annual exemption each year to reduce the taxable gain. The remaining gain would obviously be subject to CGT. There would be no stamp duty land tax (SDLT) for your nephew to pay, because the transfers are gifts for no consideration. But if afterwards he would want to buy his first home, he would not be eligible for the new SDLT first-time buyer exemption, because he already owns (part of) a property. See Chapter 3 of HMRC's guidance at: www.gov.uk/government/uploads/system/uploads/attachment_data/file/661728/8274_guidance_note_SDLT_relief_for_first_time_buyers.pdf.

145. Would I Have To Pay Additional Tax?

Question: I own a property with my ex-husband in Manchester, which I currently reside in. The estimated property value is £250,000. If I were to buy him out would I have to pay additional tax or stamp duty land tax, even though I paid this when we bought the property?

Answer: If you own no other properties and you pay him not more than £125,000, then there will be no stamp duty land tax for you to pay when you buy his half of the property from him. Any potential capital gains tax is on him, not you.

146. Will Essential Repair Costs Reduce My Tax Liability?

Question: I am selling a house which I have owned for three years in Bath, which was transferred to me by my husband. It is let in three flats. It was valued when I acquired it at £800,000, and I am selling it for £925,000 for completion of the purchase on 1 July 2018. I am 70 years old and would like clarification on the likely capital gains tax which I would be liable for. I have spent some £100,000 on essential repairs and renovations since owning the house

Answer: The answer to your question involves determining the nature of your £100,000 expenditure. If it was wholly capital expenditure, it can reduce the £125,000

capital gain to £25,000. If none or only some of it was capital expenditure then the £125,000 will not be reduced, or only partly reduced, accordingly. Look at HMRC's guidance at: www.gov.uk/hmrc-internal-manuals/property-income-manual/pim2025 and pim2030 to find out what is capital expenditure, and what is not.

147. If I Sell My Only Home Would I Be Liable To Tax?

Question: We have owned our current house (which has been our home) for the last 20 years. We are considering downsizing by buying a second property, which is in need of modernisation, with the intention of selling our home and then moving into the second property when updating is completed. Would I be liable to pay capital gains tax (CGT) on the sale of my current home?

Answer: From what you have written it would appear that you will not pay any capital gains tax (CGT) when you sell your current home, because all the gain is covered by principal private residence relief. That being so, you would not even have to put this sale on the capital gains supplementary pages of the self-assessment tax return.

148. How Can We Transfer The Property And Not Pay Tax?

Question: My husband and I bought a house specifically for our daughter to live in 12 years ago because she was expecting a baby. We paid a deposit of £50,000 and have a mortgage for the balance of £150,000. Our daughter paid all the monthly mortgage amounts and has spent approximately £50,000 on a loft extension and renovations. We are about to retire and would like our deposit back from her and transfer the house into her name. How can we prove that she has the beneficial interest to HMRC, such that if we transfer it into her name we do not pay a huge amount of capital gains tax?. There is still £80,000 outstanding on the mortgage (eight years remaining) but we could possibly borrow this to redeem it on the understanding she would re-mortgage the house, once it was in her name, and repay us. The house is currently worth approximately £450,000.

Answer: If you look at HMRC's guidance in the Capital Gains manual (at www.gov.uk/hmrc-internal-manuals/capital-gains-manual/cg70230, second bullet point) you can see that you may have an argument to say that the house has always been beneficially owned by your daughter, even though it was not originally put into writing. Furthermore, if you look at CG65406 you can see that if you put things into writing now it would help (although there are other contrary indications on the HMRC manuals). If so, merely transferring the legal ownership now to your daughter will not involve any CGT (see CG10720).

149. Gift Of Property With Mortgage

Question I own my property in Brighton and the mortgage still has 20 years until it is paid off. However, I decided to give it to my brother. He already has a flat that he pays a mortgage on. What are the tax implications?

Answer: It seems that you are giving away your main residence, so there should be no capital gains tax for you to pay, due to principal private residence relief. Since you are gifting your property to your brother for no consideration, he will have no stamp duty land tax (SDLT) to pay. However, if he takes over responsibility for the mortgage, that will be deemed as though he paid you, and he will have to pay SDLT based on the amount of the mortgage he becomes responsible for.

150. Tax Position for a Donor and Donee?

Question I have a friend who gifted a house 16 years ago to his sister. The sister now wants to transfer the property back to the brother. She is a higher rate taxpayer and the brother is a basic rate taxpayer. The property for the last 16 years was privately rented for 60% of the time and the brother lived there for the remainder of the time. What are the tax implications for both of them?

Answer: A transfer between connected persons (and brother and sister are connected persons) is deemed to take place, for capital gains tax (CGT) purposes, at today's market value (see HMRC's Capital Gains manual at CG14530). So, the sister will be deemed to have bought the house 16 years ago at its market value then and will be deemed to be selling it today at its market value today. The amount of money that changes hands is irrelevant. So, if it has gone up in value in the past 16 years, the sister will be making a capital gain, and after deducting the capital gains tax annual exemption (currently £12,000), she will have to pay 28% CGT on this gain.

151. Passing Second Home Down the Generations

Question Can I gift my second home to my daughter who will then transfer ownership in two years' time to her daughter who will then be 18?

Answer: You can certainly gift your second home to your daughter, who can transfer it to your granddaughter in two years' time. However, since it is your second home, it may not be eligible to some/any principal private residence relief, and so there may be some/a lot of capital gains tax for you to pay. When your daughter transfers in two years' time she will be in a similar situation, except that her base cost will be today's value (i.e. the market value of the property on the day it was gifted to her). Alternatively, you could gift the property to your granddaughter today. Although she is under 18, she can still be the beneficial owner of the property, but someone over 18 will have to be the legal owner.

152. Can We Transfer Properties?

Question We own six rental properties in Somerset (a couple are in our children's names, who are both under 18) and we would like to transfer them to a new limited company. I heard you can transfer your rental properties into a partnership for three years first and then transfer to a company using incorporation relief to avoid all stamp duty land tax (SDLT) and capital gains tax (CGT)?

Answer: What you are saying has become a popular quote. In theory this may work. However, there are significant details that you have 'glossed over'. Firstly, would you be eligible for CGT incorporation relief on the transfer; can your rental properties be described as a 'business'? Secondly, if HMRC challenged what you are doing on the basis that you are doing it to avoid tax, it could be that you would not get the partnership relief from SDLT that you are hoping for (FA 2003, s 75A). Thirdly, would you be able to transfer all your current mortgages into the company? There are other difficulties with what you have written. I suggest you consider first whether you can overcome these obstacles, and then speak to a tax adviser.

153. Gifting A Property To My Children

Question I have a flat in Birmingham (not my main residence) which I would like to gift to my three children in equal parts, either directly or by moving it into a company and giving them the shares. Would there be stamp duty land tax (SDLT), capital gains tax (CGT) or inheritance tax (IHT) implications in either case? The property is worth more than £350,000.

Answer: With regard to SDLT, if you gift directly to your children, there will be no SDLT for them to pay if you don't charge them anything for the purchase. However, if they want to buy a first home in the future, they will not be able to use the first-time buyers' relief because of their part ownership of this property.

If you gift to a company, the company will have to pay SDLT based on the current market value of the property, but your children will not lose their eligibility to the first-time buyers' relief because of this. For CGT purposes, you will have to pay CGT based on the difference between what you originally paid for the property and its current market value.

For IHT purposes, if you gift to them personally it will be a potentially exempt transfer, so if you live for seven years afterwards there will be no IHT for your estate. If you gift to a company, this will be a 'chargeable lifetime transfer' and assuming you have your IHT nil rate band (currently £325,000) available to you, any amount of the gift over £325,000 will be subject to an immediate 20% lifetime IHT charge.

154. Tax Position On Selling Our Jointly Owned House

Question Will I pay tax on the sale proceeds of my current house, which I have lived in since 1981 but was originally owned by my mother? My sister and I inherited it ten years ago when she died, and I have continued to live in it since. My sister and I are currently joint owners.

Answers: The fact that you lived in the house before ten years ago is not relevant. Your ownership starts from ten years ago when you inherited from your mother. You should not pay any capital gains tax (CGT) now since you have lived in the house all the period of your ownership. If your sister has also lived in the house for the past ten years, she will also pay no CGT now, like you. But if she has not lived in the house, she will pay CGT now. Her base cost will be half the probate value of the house when it was inherited ten years ago.

155. What If The Developer Pays More Than Market Value?

Question: If I sell my property which is my primary residence to a developer and they pay 25% above the market value for the property, do I have to pay tax on the amount that they pay in excess of the market value, or is all of it tax-free as it is being paid for my primary residence?

Answer: If you have lived in your property as your main residence all the period of your ownership, so that it is fully eligible for principal private residence relief, you do not have to pay any capital gains tax on its sale, even if the purchaser is paying above market value.

156. What Is My Tax Position On The Property Sale?

Question: My daughter and I owned a property brought for my daughter to live in and she lived there for ten years before we sold the property. The deposit was paid by me. I received no income. When we sold the property we split the selling value 50:50 between me and my daughter. What is the capital gains tax (CGT) implication for me?

Answer: CGT is dependent on beneficial ownership. See HMRC's Capital Gains manual at www.gov.uk/hmrc-internal-manuals/capital-gains-manual/cg70230. Since you paid the deposit, and you received half the sales proceeds, this would indicate that you had half the beneficial ownership, and consequently you should be liable to CGT on half the gain. But since your daughter was the only one who lived in the property, this would suggest that she was the sole beneficial owner. In your scenario, I do not know whether you were the sole legal owner, or your daughter, or both of you were joint legal owners. I think you should ask a tax adviser.

157. Will HMRC Think My Offer Is Illegal?

Question: My Dad just passed away and my mum has gone into a care home. As my husband and I have not bought our own house we are thinking of buying their home. The house is in Scotland. Currently the market value is £300,000; however, with the slump in the oil industry and Covid-19 and the fact that the house is a little run down (e.g. kitchen cupboards broken, main shower not working, boiler does not produce hot water and carpets are worn) we are first time cash buyers and can afford to offer only approximately £240,000. My mum has plenty of money in shares for her own care. Initially my sister's Power of Attorney was all for £240,000.

Having previously looked into buying a house through auction, I think this offer is fair. However today my sister's Power of Attorney has said the High Street estate agent laughed at this offer and said it should not be sold for less than £300,000 or she could be investigated for not doing right by mum. Please could you tell me it there anything illegal in my offer? Is the estate agent only after her own pocket?

Answer: You are allowed to buy this house from your mum for whatever the family agrees to. HMRC do not come into this here. The amount of money that you actually pay will be the amount that you Land & Buildings Transaction Tax (LBTT) on.

However for capital gains tax purposes, your mother is deemed to be selling it at its market value, and you are deemed to be buying it at the same amount. See HMRC's Capital Gains manual (www.gov.uk/hmrc-internal-manuals/capital-gains-manual/cg14530). This is because you and your mum are connected persons. But if, as is quite likely, your mum has lived in her house as her main residence all the time she owned the house, she will not pay any CGT when she sells to you, even at a higher figure, because all her capital gain is covered by principal private residence relief.

So there is nothing illegal in your offer. You just need to sort out your sister.

158. Tax Implications Of Gifting Property Or Cash

Question: I have savings for my two daughters, and as interest rates are so low in their savings account I think it would be best to invest in property in Manchester instead. I've read a lot about this but am unsure what is gifting and what is selling. For example, my eldest is 18 in two years' time.

My idea is to buy the property now with a buy-to-let mortgage and when she is 18 transfer to her name. If she is in education she can continue to rent the property out. If she is working she can live there and take on a mortgage or transfer the mortgage into her name. When her sister turns 18 three years later the plan would be to add her name onto the mortgage and deeds.

Should something happen in between and we cannot afford to upkeep the property, we would sell and the funds split between both children. So I'm unsure whether this is a gift or a sale and what the tax implications are for both. I am a higher taxpayer and the mortgage would be around £125,000, with the property worth around £165,000.

Answer: When you transfer to your first daughter when she becomes 18, this could mean capital gains tax (CGT) for you, if the property has gone up in value since you bought it. Similarly, when the second daughter becomes 18 and the first transfers (say) a half of the property to her, this could mean CGT for the first daughter, if the property has gone up in value from the time she acquired it. If something should happen in between and the property is sold, then whoever is the owner at that point will have to calculate the increase in value between the sale and the amount they acquired it for, and pay CGT accordingly. If the property is sold and the funds split between both children, the splitting of the funds is irrelevant for tax purposes (in theory, IHT could be relevant to these transactions - but very unlikely). It is unlikely that stamp duty land tax will impact on your daughters - due to first time buyers relief.

159. What Tax Implications If I Sign My House Over To My Daughter?

Question: I own a house in Birmingham worth (approximately) £380,000. My daughter owns a flat in Coventry worth (approximately) £190,000, which she doesn't live in but rents out. If she sells the flat and gives me the proceeds (which I add to buy a retirement flat) and I sign the house over to her (she would otherwise inherit half the property value eventually), what would be the tax implications? I don't think inheritance tax (IHT) would be an issue as I have a double allowance.

Answer:
If your house was your principal private residence there should be no capital gains tax (CGT) for you to pay. Your daughter may be liable to CGT on the sale of her flat, if £190,000 is more than she originally paid for it. If the £190,000 is a deemed payment by your daughter for your house, then (see HMRC's Stamp Duty Land Tax manual at www.gov.uk/hmrc-internal-manuals/stamp-duty-land-tax-manual/sdltm00055) she will pay 3% SDLT if she owns another house, and no SDLT if she doesn't. The £380,000 that you are giving her, less £190,000 that she is giving you, will be a potentially exempt transfer (PET) for IHT purposes.

160. Splitting Title And Selling: What's The Best Thing To Do?

Question: My son and wife and two children live in the self-contained ground floor area of a large house. My daughter and I live in the first floor area. Each dwelling has its own council tax and utility bills. The house is owned by myself and my son and daughter as joint tenants. My question is: will we be liable for any capital gains tax (CGT) if we split the title and sell? The ground floor dwelling is now too small for my son and his family so they need to move on. My daughter and I would ideally like to move to the ground floor. Or is it more prudent for my daughter and I to stay where we are in the first floor flat and put the new lease/title in our name, and for my son to put the new lease/title in his name and then sell just the ground floor flat?

Answer: I suggest you get tax advice about possibly implementing the exchange arrangements outlined in HMRC's guidance at https://www.gov.uk/hmrc-internal-manuals/capital-gains-manual/cg65150p, so that your son can have full ownership over the ground floor part, and you and your daughter can have full ownership over the first floor part (this is not the relief described in HMRC's Capital Gains Tax manual at https://www.gov.uk/hmrc-internal-manuals/capital-gains-manual/cg73000.) Then each part can be disposed of in a tax efficient way, using principal private residence relief, according to your family plans.

161. When Will Capital Gains Tax Be Calculated From?

Question: My friend lived in her house for 30 years. She then married and moved overseas, letting it last year. Will she now be liable for capital gains tax (CGT) for the whole 30 plus years, or just since April 2020?

Answer: Since she is now non-UK resident; assuming she stays non-UK resident for five consecutive tax years, she will only be liable for the gain from April 2015 onwards. However, she lived in the house as her main residence until 2019, so these years will be exempt. The last nine months of ownership are also exempt (final period exemption) (see HMRC's Capital Gains manual at www.gov.uk/hmrc-internal-manuals/capital-gains-manual/cg65070.

162. What Is My Tax Position?

Question: I'm buying a plot of land and building two houses on it. I want to sell one to my daughter at cost (or even less than cost). What is the capital gains tax (CGT) position? I realise I must survive for seven years to mitigate any liability for inheritance tax, if I transfer at less than cost.

Answer: The tax rules state that any transfer to a connected person (e.g. a daughter) is deemed to be at present market value for CGT purposes, irrespective of what is actually paid between the two parties. So if you do what you are planning, you will be liable to tax, because presumably the market value of the completed house will be more than the land cost and building costs. From a tax perspective, you are best giving or lending your daughter cash to: (a) purchase the land; and (b) do the building herself. However, this may not be the most practical solution.

163. Tenant Wants To Purchase The Property

Question: I own a second property, which I rent to my son. He wishes to join the property market but can't afford a mortgage. He has proposed to buy the rental property he occupies by paying me a fixed sum each month for a pre-defined percentage ownership of the rental property. He will continue to pay me rent on the percentage I still own. My questions are: (1) Do I pay capital gains tax (CGT) or income tax on this fixed monthly sum? (2) If it is CGT to pay but the annual sum paid each year is below the personal CGT allowance, do I avoid paying CGT year on year?

Answer: The money he pays you is subject to CGT. If you would make a new contract each month, then each month would be a new sale, and would trigger a small capital gain. Because CGT is dependent on the contract (see HMRC's Capital Gains manual:

www.gov.uk/hmrc-internal-manuals/capital-gains-manual/cg14260). But if instead you had only one contract, which stated that the property is being transferred and paid for a bit each month, the whole amount would be subject to CGT immediately. If you choose to make a new contract each month, and the sum total of the capital gains is below the CGT annual exemption, it is possible to avoid paying CGT year on year.

164. Selling My Home And Moving In With My Husband

Question: A couple who married five years ago and have not yet sold their properties to live together, have lived separately. After five years of living separately the wife who had mobility problems due to an operation (and other problems) is now mobile enough to move in with the husband and sell her home. She has genuinely been living in her own home, has bills to prove it, diaries to show down to so much detail she knows which nights she spent at her property (the vast majority of them). The husband has been living in his own home. She is concerned that a taxable capital gain will arise for the married period of ownership (five years) as a proportion of total ownership as HMRC will argue that point under HMRC's Capital Gains manual (www.gov.uk/hmrc-internal-manuals/capital-gains-manual/cg64525). Are they both entitled to each of their PPR and do you feel it would be a successful argument with HMRC?

Answer: If you look at HMRC's Capital Gains manual (at www.gov.uk/hmrc-internal-manuals/capital-gains-manual/cg65300) it states: 'Spouses or civil partners who are living together can have only one only or main residence between them, TCGA92/S222 (6)', but 'spouses or civil partners who are separated are each entitled to relief on their own only or main residence'. The definition of 'living together' and 'separated' is given at CG22070. It seems to me that from what you have described HMRC would argue that this couple fell into the 'living together' category, and consequently would only be eligible to one PPR between them (see CG64525).

165. Removing A Name From Property Title Deeds

Question: My wife and I own a buy-to-let leasehold flat in Leeds as joint tenants. Can I remove my name from the title deeds so that my wife receives the full rental income? Would there be any tax implications for us such as capital gains tax (CGT) or stamp duty land tax (SDLT)?

Answer: You can move the house from being owned in joint names, into her sole legal name. Since you are husband and wife (I presume living together), there will be no CGT. If there is no payment from her to you, and if there is no mortgage (or even if there is a mortgage, if the responsibility for the mortgage does not change) there will be no SDLT. See HMRC's Stamp Duty Land Tax manual at www.gov.uk/hmrc-internal-manuals/stamp-duty-land-tax-manual/sdltm00330a.

166. Can Dad Sell A Mortgaged Flat To Me?

Question: My dad bought a property for £450,000 in 2006. He has since extended the property into three flats and refinanced several years ago. The three flats are now worth £1.4 million in total. He wishes to retire and sell/gift one to me for below market value. With £625,000 left on the mortgage, is this even possible? The flat has a market value of £450,000 and he wishes to sell it to me for around £300,000. His aim I guess is to avoid a huge capital gains tax (CGT) bill.

Answer: Your father can certainly sell/gift one of the flats to you. But presumably he would need to sort things out with his mortgage lender. He can charge you £300,000, or £450,000, or any different amount, or gift for nothing; it makes no difference from a CGT perspective. Since he is your father, for CGT purposes when he transfers to you he is deemed to be selling for its present market value (i.e. £450,000).

167. Putting My Current Properties Into A New Company?

Question: I sold property and invested into a limited company. Unfortunately, the limited company failed. Can the money invested be recovered in any way? When I sell something in the future at a gain, can capital gains tax (CGT) be offset? Can any deductions be made on my normal income tax returns? It would really help in deciding if I should put my current properties into new limited company, with the CGT offset for past loss.

Answer: If the shares have become of negligible value, they can be treated as a capital loss, and offset against current or future capital gains; see HMRC's Capital Gains manual here: www.gov.uk/hmrc-internal-manuals/capital-gains-manual/cg13120p. Under certain circumstances, such a loss can instead be set against income; see HMRC's Venture Capital Scheme manual here: www.gov.uk/hmrc-internal-manuals/venture-capital-schemes-manual/vcm70000.

168. Splitting Title And Selling: What's Should I Do?

Question: My son and wife and two children live in the self-contained ground floor area of a large house. My daughter and I live in the first floor area. Each dwelling has its own council tax and utility bills. The house is owned by myself and my son and daughter as joint tenants.

My question is: will we be liable for any capital gains tax (CGT) if we split the title and sell? The ground floor dwelling is now too small for my son and his family so they need to move on. My daughter and I would ideally like to move to the ground floor.

Or is it more prudent for my daughter and I to stay where we are in the first floor flat and put the new lease/title in our name, and for my son to put the new lease/title in his name and then sell just the ground floor flat?

Answer: I suggest you get tax advice about possibly implementing the exchange arrangements outlined in HMRC's guidance at https://www.gov.uk/hmrc-internal-manuals/capital-gains-manual/cg65150p, so that your son can have full ownership over the ground floor part, and you and your daughter can have full ownership over the first floor part (this is not the relief described in HMRC's Capital Gains Tax manual at https://www.gov.uk/hmrc-internal-manuals/capital-gains-manual/cg73000.) Then each part can be disposed of in a tax efficient way, using principal private residence relief, according to your family plans.

169. When Will Capital Gains Tax Be Calculated From?

Question: My friend lived in her house for 30 years. She then married and moved overseas, letting it last year. Will she now be liable for capital gains tax (CGT) for the whole 30 plus years, or just since April 2020?

Answer: Since she is now non-UK resident; assuming she stays non-UK resident for five consecutive tax years, she will only be liable for the gain from April 2015 onwards. However, she lived in the house as her main residence until 2019, so these years will be exempt. The last nine months of ownership are also exempt (final period exemption) (see HMRC's Capital Gains manual at www.gov.uk/hmrc-internal-manuals/capital-gains-manual/cg65070.

170. **Can I Sell One Of My Properties At Less Than Cost?**

    Question: I'm buying a plot of land and building two houses on it. I want to sell one to my daughter at cost (or even less than cost). What is the capital gains tax (CGT) position? I realise I must survive for seven years to mitigate any liability for inheritance tax, if I transfer at less than cost.

    Answer: The tax rules state that any transfer to a connected person (e.g. a daughter) is deemed to be at present market value for CGT purposes, irrespective of what is actually paid between the two parties. So if you do what you are planning, you will be liable to tax, because presumably the market value of the completed house will be more than the land cost and building costs. From a tax perspective, you are best giving or lending your daughter cash to: (a) purchase the land; and (b) do the building herself. However, this may not be the most practical solution.

171. **Tax Position If He Gifts Me His Buy To Let Property?**

    Question: My older brother now lives in the USA and he is gifting me his buy to let property in the UK. I need to know will I or he need to pay capital gains tax (CGT) on the property?

    Answer: Your brother will need to pay UK capital gains tax based on the increase in value from the date he bought the property, or the increase in value from April 2015, whichever date is later. Since he is now gifting the property to his brother, he has to use today's market value as his 'sale proceeds'.

172. **Selling A Property We Haven't Occupied**

    Question: I own two rental income properties. My wife and I live in armed forces accommodation and my wife owns one rental property of her own. I am thinking about selling one of my properties to buy another higher value property. What would this mean for capital gains tax (CGT) purposes now and potentially in the future when my wife and I both own our own home that we live in? I am aware of the CGT exemption for selling your 'home'; would this apply in this scenario? Further, if it does and I claimed the sale of this property was my 'home' to not pay CGT this time, how would it affect my wife and I when we do own our own house that we live in and then choose to move house?

    Answer: Principal private residence (PPR) relief from CGT is potentially available for someone in job related accommodation (see HMRC's Capital Gains manual at www.gov.uk/hmrc-internal-manuals/capital-gains-manual/cg64555). However, one of the requirements is that the person intends to occupy the property as their main residence. This does not seem to be your scenario. So the sale of this rental property will be assessable to CGT in the normal way and any future home that you lived in as your main residence will be eligible for PPR relief.

173. Transferring Beneficial Ownership In A Flat

Question: I would like to enquire about the feasibility, and tax implications, of transferring beneficial ownership regarding my particular circumstances. I own a flat in Liverpool, which I live in as a joint tenant together with my mum. We are both also on the mortgage deed. I would like to transfer beneficial ownership, so my mum holds 99%, and I hold 1%.

Among the key questions I have at this stage is whether there would be any stamp duty land tax (SDLT) implications in this scenario. As my mum is already on the mortgage deed, and I presume jointly liable for the entirety of the remaining mortgage, I can't see what the chargeable consideration would be in this case by me transferring any amount of beneficial ownership. Would there be any capital gains tax (CGT) implications in view of the fact that we are both already legal owners of the property? What are the implications of having this 99%/1% beneficial ownership structure when it comes to any future sale of the property whilst we are both alive and in the case of one of us passing?

Answer: HMRC makes an assumption in its SDLT manual at SDLTM00330a (https://tinyurl.com/HMRC-SDLTM00330a, Example 3) that if ownership of the property is being transferred, mortgage responsibility is also being transferred. This assumption is highly questionable.

Just to be on the safe side, it is worth stipulating in the document transferring beneficial ownership from you to your mother, that there is no change in mortgage responsibility. Then there will be no SDLT on this transfer. However, there will be CGT on this transfer, as CGT follows beneficial ownership (see HMRC's Capital Gains manual at CG70230) (https://tinyurl.com/HMRC-CG00330a), and you are disposing of beneficial ownership of 49% of the property. The legal ownership is irrelevant here. When the property is sold in the future, your mother will receive 99% of the sale proceeds, and you 1%. When your mother dies, 99% of this property will be included in her estate for inheritance tax purposes.

174. How Can I Minimise CGT On The Sale Of A Flat?

Question: My brother and I jointly inherited my parents' house on their death. My brother has lived in the house for 69 years and still does. I have since married and purchased my own property. We have spent years renovating my brother's house, converting it into two flats, which now have separate values due to size and garden. We plan to sell the two flats. How can I minimise my capital gains tax (CGT) liability, notwithstanding my brother will not be liable, as this is his only residence? Do we need to re-register the properties under different names, with me taking on the lower valued flat?

Answer: There is a relief from CGT for two joint owners of a property who wish to split up and not incur any CGT, as per HMRC's Capital Gains manual at CG73000 (https://tinyurl.com/9vcpa8). However, it does not apply when it involves the main residence of one or both of the two parties. There is another relief that applies when two individuals swap rights in each other's main residence: see HMRC's guidance at CG65150P (https://tinyurl.com/4m535fek). But in your scenario, only one of the two parties is using the property as his main residence, so I do not know how you can minimise your capital gain. It appears that you have jointly owned the property for a long time. Therefore in your CGT computation, make sure you use the March 1982 valuation if it is later and higher than the original acquisition cost.

175. Is CGT Payable On A Deposit?

Question: An exchange on a property took place in the tax year 2019/20. The buyer failed to complete and is suing the seller for the return of the deposit, which was released to the seller on exchange. If the case does not come before the court in the current tax year, the seller may have to return the money in the following tax year, depending on the outcome. Does the seller have to pay capital gains tax (CGT) on the deposit prior to the outcome of the case? Is it payable in the year in which it would become due now, even if their right to it is disputed by the failed buyer?

Answer: Please read HMRC's Capital Gains manual at CG12340, CG12350 second bullet point, CG12940 and CG12952. It seems to me that the seller is liable to CGT if they keep the deposit. See CG12960 about when the CGT is due.

176. Any Tax Liability If Removed From Mortgage?

Question: I jointly own a buy-to-let property with my father and brother. We have done so for the past seven years. We have a mortgage on it, and the property has increased in value considerably since we purchased it. I wish to remove myself from the mortgage and property ownership so that it will then be owned just by my father and my brother. I wish to receive no monetary value for this departure - the equity will simply remain in the property and belong to those still named on the mortgage. Can you please advise whether I would be liable to pay capital gains tax in this instance, even though I will not be receiving anything in terms of cash?

Answer: When you withdraw from ownership of the property, you are effectively gifting to your father and brother. Additionally, since they are your relatives, this is a transfer to a connected person. If you look at HMRC's Capital Gains manual at CG14530 it states that you are deemed to transfer to them at market value. So you are making a capital gain, even though you are not receiving any payment.

177. How Much Principal Private Residence Relief Can I Claim?

Question: Does HMRC check if I owned another property during the time I owned the flat I am now selling and have capital gains tax (CGT) to pay on? I got married after four years and moved in with my husband, and my mother-in-law lived in my flat, but the council tax was still in my name there. Can I claim the flat as my main residence when mother-in-law was there, as the council tax bill was still in my name and the flat was not rented out, as she stayed there rent-free?

Answer: You can claim CGT principal private residence relief when selling your flat for the period when you actually lived there, but not for the period when you lived somewhere else. The fact that your mother-in-law lived there doesn't count (there used to be a dependant relative relief, but this is almost certainly not relevant to you, because the dependant relative had to be in the property in 1988).

178. **The Tax Position When Gifting Mortgaged Properties**

Question: How can I avoid or reduce capital gains tax (CGT) when gifting mortgaged rental property to my son, who will live in it as his principal private residence, and another property to my daughter, who will rent it out?

Answer: If you read HMRC's Capital Gains manual at CG14480P, it states that when you transfer property to your children, you are deemed for CGT purposes to transfer at present market value. Most likely, that will trigger CGT. You could try transferring a bit each year between you and your spouse (if that is applicable) using your CGT annual exemption (currently £12,300), but this is not really a practical solution. You could transfer to a trust, wait three months, and then transfer the trust to your children. However: (a) this requires professional guidance; and (b) it will clash with the possibility of claiming principal private residence relief, so it is not useful for your son.

179. **Changing Houses: What Taxes?**

Question: My old house in Birmingham was my main residence from April 2014 to May 2019. The old house cost £207,000, and it was purchased solely in my name. I have rented out my old house from May 2019 to date as I was waiting for the housing market to get better before selling it. I purchased my new house (my current main residence) in May 2019 for £350,000, and I paid stamp duty land tax (SDLT) of £18,080, which included additional SDLT. What I plan to do now is to sell my old house for £300,000 to my own new limited company, which will net me a profit of £93,000. The company has me and my wife as the directors. My questions are: (1) Will I get charged any capital gains tax (CGT), considering that this was my main residence? (2) Will I get my additional SDLT that I paid for the new house reimbursed? My limited company plans to rent out the property. (3) Am I doing everything legally?

Answer: Dealing with your questions in turn: (1) Let's say you sell to your company in August 2021. The period from May 2019 to August 2021 (i.e. 27 months) will be taxable, less the last nine months' final period exemption (i.e. 18 months). Ignoring any enhancement expenditure and incidental costs of purchase and sale, the capital gain of £93,000 is spread over 88 months of ownership (i.e. April 2014 to August 2021), and the gain per month is multiplied by 18 months, so you will have a taxable gain of around £19,000.

After deducting your capital gains tax (CGT) annual exemption (AE) of £12,300, you will have to pay CGT on £6,700. This assumes that £300,000 is the actual current market value of the house. If you first transferred to your wife before selling to your company, she may also have her AE to offset against the gain. (2) You can claim a refund for the extra 3% SDLT paid. (3) Whilst I am not a lawyer, you appear to be doing everything legally.

180. **Splitting Our Home Into Flats: What Tax Liability Will Arise?**

Question: My wife and I have lived in our home in Bristol for 20 years, and I want to split our home into two flats and sell one of the flats to our LLP. Will we incur stamp duty land tax (SDLT) and capital gains tax (CGT)?

Answer: Look at HMRC's Partnerships manual at PM131430 (tinyurl.com/rs6cf9vy), where it states: "Capital gains: The transfer of a business from a general partnership to an [limited liability partnership (LLP)] will not constitute a disposal by the partners of their interests in the original partnership's assets", and "Stamp duty land tax: The transfer of chargeable interests to the LLP will be exempted from charge if certain conditions are met. Please refer to SDLTM33690 for full details". The reason for this is, as stated at PM131450: "All the activities of the LLP are treated as being carried on in partnership by its members (and not by the LLP as such)", and: "Most LLPs are transparent for tax purposes".

181. Overseas Owner Of UK Property: The Tax Position On Selling

Question: Last year my wife and I took residency in Spain. We have two properties in the UK currently rented out. My main residence, which I bought in 1974 for £7,000, is now worth about £180,000 and has been rented out for 18 months to date. However, when the current tenant moves out it will need upgrading, so it may be cheaper to sell it on as is. My question is, if I sell this property for £180,000 and buy a cheaper property for, say, £140,000, will I pay capital gains tax (CGT) on the difference? And if so, how much?

Answer: If you sell the ex-main residence for £180,000, you will be liable to capital gains tax (CGT) on its sale; it is not relevant that you are buying another property for £140,000. The CGT liability is based on the difference between £180,000 and the value of the property in March 1982 (not the £7,000 figure you paid for it in 1974). For argument's sake, let's say the March 1982 value was £10,000, so your capital gain is £170,000. Let's also assume you sell in March 2022, so you will have owned the house for forty years since March 1982. This equates to a gain of £4,250 per year. The last nine months of ownership of a main residence are exempt from CGT, as is all the period you lived in the house as your main residence. Let's say March 2022 will be two years since you moved out and started to rent it out. So, your CGT liability will be 24 months less nine months, which is 15 months. If the gain is £4,250 per year, your taxable capital gain for 15 months will be £5,312. This is less than the CGT annual exemption, which is currently £12,300. So you would have no CGT to pay.

182. Transferring The Family Home From Single To Joint Siblings

Question: If a sibling has the family home in Liverpool in her single name (mortgage-free), and she transfers it to include herself and one or two other siblings as joint owners, what are the implications for capital gains tax (CGT) and stamp duty land tax (SDLT) purposes now and further down the line; and for inheritance tax purposes (IHT) when any of them die?

Answer: Any transfer between siblings is deemed to be at market value for CGT purposes (see HMRC's Capital Gains manual: tinyurl.com/2wy9bkab). Let's say the sibling acquired the house for £200,000, and now it is worth £290,000. If she makes two other siblings joint owners together with her, she has effectively given away two-thirds of the house, so her capital gain will be two-thirds of £90,000, which is £60,000.

However, if she has lived in the house as her main residence, she will have principal private residence relief to reduce her CGT exposure. If the transfer to the other siblings is a gift for no consideration, there will be no SDLT liability. After the transfer, each one will own one-third of the house, so this will be included in their estate when they die. If the donor sibling does not live for seven years after the date of the gift, the value of the whole house will be included in her estate for IHT purposes.

183. Do I Set Any Selling And Capital Work Costs Against Tax?

Question: My wife and I bought a property together five years ago for £123,000. My wife died two years ago and I was the sole beneficiary of her will. My son lived in it but has very recently passed away. I will sell the property most probably in this tax year for (say) £155,000. I believe I can claim any selling and capital work costs for tax purposes, but as my late wife and I owned the property jointly can I reduce my capital gain to reflect this and if so over what period does my gain apply (e.g. the period since my wife's death?).

Answer:
Your base cost for the 50% of the house you bought five years ago is £123,000/2 = £61,500. When your wife died two years ago, you inherited her 50% of the house at probate value (i.e. the market value at the date of death). Let's suppose the probate value of her 50% of the house was (£142,000/2) = £71,000. So your combined base cost for both halves is £61,500 + £71,000 = £132,500. If you sell for £155,000, your capital gain will be £22,500. From this figure you can deduct selling and capital costs, as you have written, and also your capital gains tax annual exemption of £12,300.

184. What Are Our Tax Positions On Gifting Money For A Property?

Question: We bought a house 10 years ago as a place for my son and his family to live. The cost was £250,000. Last year my son bought the house from us and the house was valued at £330,000 but we gifted him £32,000 so that he could afford the mortgage. Was this OK or do we need to also declare the £32,000 as capital gains?

Answer: The gift of £32,000 is irrelevant to the capital gains matter. However, since the house was worth £80,000 more when you disposed of it, than when you acquired it, you have made a capital gain of £80,000. This is because any transfer to a connected person (e.g. a son) is deemed by the tax rules to be at present market value.

185. Is There A Capital Gains Tax Liability On This Property Sale?

Question: My mum and dad are in the process of selling their old home. They lived there from 1978 until 2008 and since then it has been used as a storage building for my dad and also he has rented it out but only for short periods, possibly for two years. The past year it has been totally empty. He has a mortgage of £105,000 on it and sold it for £240,000. Will he have to pay tax on this, and if so, how much?

Answer: Your parents owned the house for 43 years, of which it was their home for 30 years. The last 13 years are taxable, less the final period exemption of nine months. Let's say they bought it for £111,000, so that it has gone up £129,000 over 43 years. This is a gain of £3,000 per year.

The capital gain will be 12.25 years multiplied by £3,000 = £36,750. If your parents jointly owned the house, each would have a capital gain of £18,375, and the CGT annual exemption of £12,300 against their half of the capital gain, resulting in a taxable capital gain of £6,075. Obviously, you will have to adjust my figures, taking into account the actual purchase price.

186. **Can We Estimate Costs In The Absence Of Receipts?**

Question: We are selling a property which will attract capital gains tax (CGT) and have made improvements to it over the time that we have owned it (23 years). Unfortunately, we have lost some invoices for the improvements and have no proof of what we paid. Can we estimate the costs incurred, or will we have to forego the claims?

Answer: You can estimate the capital expenditure that you have put into the property over the 23 years, and claim a reduction of the capital gain due to enhancement expenditure. However, you must realise that if HMRC should question you and ask to see proof, you will be in a bit of a difficult position.

187. **Sale Of Property To Tenant: How Do I Work Out The Capital Gains Tax?**

Question: I have a property in Birmingham that I bought in August 2011 for £138,500. The property has been continuously rented out since April 2012. It is valued at £175,000 and my tenants wish to purchase it. How do I work out how much capital gains tax (CGT) I'm due to pay? What factors are involved in calculating the amount due?

Answer: Very simply, your capital gain is £175,000 - £138,500 = £36,500. If you paid stamp duty land tax, estate agents fees, and solicitors fees when you purchased in 2011, and if you have to pay solicitors fees when you sell, you can deduct these from the £36,500. If you haven't used it so far in this tax year, you can also deduct the capital gains tax annual exemption (currently £12,300). The resulting capital gain is added on to your other income. Any part of the capital gain that falls below the higher rate threshold is taxed at 18%, and any part above the threshold is taxed at 28%.

188. **When Should I Nominate My Main Residence?**

Question: I want to sell a property I bought 19 years ago, having lived there eight years before I bought it and four years after. I have let it for approximately nine out of the 19 years I have owned it. I would like to know if I can nominate it as my main residence and how private residence relief is calculated. Can I claim my contribution towards improvement works as an expense?

Answer: If you lived in the property as your main residence for four years after you bought the property, you do not now need to nominate the property as your main residence; it was automatically designated your main residence for those years, as per HMRC's Capital Gains manual at CG64545 (https://tinyurl.com/y7whs7sm).

Unfortunately, the eight years you occupied the property before you bought it will not count; see CG64930 (https://tinyurl.com/HMRC-CG64930).

Any enhancement expenditure you put into improving the property (if still in existence) that you did not at the time offset against your rental income, can be offset against the capital gain. You take the capital gain (call it £X), deduct your enhancement expenditure, resulting in £Y, then divide £Y by 19 to find the gain per year (call it £Z). You are entitled to four years' relief for when you lived there, plus the last nine months' of ownership (assuming the four years and last nine months do not overlap). Then you deduct 4.75 * £Z relief from £Y to find your final taxable gain.

189. How Can He Avoid Capital Gains Tax On The Gifts Of Leases?

Question: My father-in-law owns six flats with long leases (999 years) on them with a peppercorn ground rent. The flats have tenants in them paying rent. He wants to gift the leases to the flats to his two children (i.e. three flats each) but avoid capital gains tax (CGT). Is this possible?

Answer: In short, it is not easy to avoid CGT on gifting the flats to his children. If he waits until he dies to leave the flats as an inheritance, there will be no CGT, but there will be inheritance tax. If he is married, it may be possible to avoid CGT. There may also be a possibility to avoid CGT by gifting to a discretionary trust. But both of these 'strategies' require advice from a tax adviser, and even where possible, both are limited in scope.

190. My Son Wants To Buy My House Tax Efficiently

Question: My son wants to buy my house in Manchester. A surveyor has valued it at £500,000, and I am happy to loan him £200,000 until he sells, or I need the money. He has about £50,000 and will need a mortgage for the rest (he has an income of over £50,000 per annum). What is the best way to proceed for tax purposes?

Answer: However much he pays you for the house, for capital gains tax (CGT) purposes, you are deemed to transfer to him at today's market value, pursuant to HMRC's Capital Gains manual at CG14530. However, if you have always lived in the house as your main residence, this will not trigger any CGT for you. But he will need to pay stamp duty land tax (SDLT) based on the amount he actually pays you. See HMRC's Stamp Duty Land Tax manual at SDLTM00055 for how much SDLT he will have to pay. It will probably be to his advantage if completion is before 30 June 2021. He may also be eligible for SDLT first time buyer's relief, as can be seen in HMRC's SDLT for first time buyers guidance note (see https://tinyurl.com/j2uav28y).

191. When Does CGT Kick In: At Assignment Price Or Selling Price?

Question: I have exchanged on an off-plan flat in Burnley and would like to assign it before completion to my daughter, who is a first-time non-resident buyer. Whilst she need not pay any stamp duty land tax (SDLT) etc., will she be liable to pay capital gains tax (CGT) if she sells after two or three years to fund her university education? If so, would the CGT be applied to the full selling price (as it is a gift) or only applied to the gains after market value at the time of assignment? For example, if I buy it for £250,000, assign it when it's worth £260,000, and she sells it two years later at £300,000, how much would the CGT be?

Answer: When you assign this property to your daughter, she is deemed to acquire it at market value, which, here, is £260,000. If afterwards, she sells it for £300,000, she will be liable to CGT on a capital gain of £40,000. See the end of the first paragraph of HMRC's Capital Gains manual at CG14530. When you assign to your daughter, I assume you do so for no consideration, so there is no SDLT for her to pay.

192. Sell Both Properties As A Job Lot Or Separately?

Question: I have a large house, a very large garden and a holiday cottage within the garden. The cottage is rented out as a furnished holiday let. These are for sale as a job lot, or alternatively I am happy to split the title and sell at the same time, as two separate sales. What are the tax implications? I think there is 10% capital gains tax on the cottage only. Is this correct and is it the case no matter which way I sell?

Answer: The capital gains tax (CGT) rate for the house, garden and holiday cottage is 18% for a basic rate taxpayer and 28% for a higher rate taxpayer, because it is residential property. However, if you live in the house as your main residence, it is likely that a part (or even all) of the capital gain on the house and garden will be exempt due to principal private residence (PPR) relief. As for the holiday cottage, it appears that you have not lived in it but only rented it out. If so, PPR relief will not be available. However, if this is the only property that you rent out as a furnished holiday letting, and if you fulfil the conditions for business asset disposal relief, you could be eligible for a 10% CGT rate.

193. Paying Half Of My Parent's House Purchase

Question: My parents would like to move near us in Manchester but cannot afford property prices. We are happy to pay half the value of the house. We already own our house. What are the implications for the purposes of stamp duty land tax (SDLT), capital gains tax (CGT) etc.? Could we put this into our children's names? My parents are over 80 years old, so they need to think about inheritance (two sons) and funding a care home. What should we do?

Answer: You would be better off lending or gifting the money (half the cost of the new house) directly to your parents, and letting them buy the house in their own names. Regarding putting half (or all) of the house into your children's names, it will affect their entitlement in the future to first-time buyer's relief from SDLT. Furthermore, when your parents finish living in the house, either because they die or they sell it, if it is in their own name, there will be no CGT. But if it is the names of your children, there will be CGT when it is sold to a third party. If it is in the name of your parents, the residence nil rate band should be available to mitigate any inheritance tax liability.

194. Can I Offset A Loss In My Self-Assessment?

Question: I re-mortgaged a buy-to-let (BTL) property and extracted equity to purchase another off-plan property. This off-plan development went bust, and I lost the deposit. Can I make an allowance of this loss against the BTL property I used to finance this failed investment, either in a self-assessment return against rental income or in the future when I sell against capital gains?

Answer: Assuming that when you purchased your rights in this off-plan development you acquired an asset that had a market value, and that now it has become of negligible value, you can claim a negligible value capital loss as per HMRC's Capital Gains manual (at CG13120p, see https://tinyurl.com/pye2jth9). This means that if, in the future, you make a capital gain, you can use this brought forward capital loss to reduce the capital gain.

195. Which Valuation Report Should Be Used?

Question: We purchased a unit, and exchange of contracts was in April 2013, with the purchase price of £403,000 (off-plan). The unit was completed in January 2016. We requested a valuation for the unit to be done on 25 October 2017. The market value was £560,000, with the valuation date back on 6 April 2015. Could this valuation report for rebasing the price help us for capital gains tax (CGT) purposes?

Answer: The amount that the taxpayer actually spent is the figure used in the CGT computation, pursuant to HMRC's Capital Gains manual at CG15150 (tinyurl.com/a2ft48ph). The fact that the asset was revalued later will not make a difference to the computation unless the taxpayer actually spent more money on enhancing the asset.

196. Transfer Of Benefit From Properties To Partner

Question: I solely own five buy-to-let properties. I want to transfer 95% of the benefit from two properties to my civil partner, along with the associated income tax. Can I just create a declaration of trust and send this with form 17 to HMRC? Will this transfer the tax liability to him and not create capital gains tax (CGT) for me from the transfer? I have seen various things on HMRC's website that indicate I can't do this (something to do with the 'settlements' legislation), but lots on the web indicates that I can.

Answer: If you are going to continue to be the sole legal owner of the two properties, you do not need a Form 17. All you need is a valid declaration of trust transferring ownership of 95% of the properties to your partner, as per HMRC's Trusts, Settlements and Estates manual at TSEM9922 (tinyurl.com/4j6sxkek). The declaration of trust does not need to be submitted to HMRC unless they ask for it. TCGA 1992, s 58 states that if you are civil partners living together, there will be no CGT for you to pay on this transfer (www.gov.uk/hmrc-internal-manuals/capital-gains-manual/cg22000).

197. Can Product Fees Be Capitalised?

Question: If a property is mortgage-free and then re-mortgaged for loan, should the mortgage fee (product fee) be capitalised?

Answer: See HMRC's Capital Gains manual (tinyurl.com/c5ct268k), where it states: "Costs of arranging a mortgage: Fees of building societies, solicitors and valuers and any other costs of arranging a mortgage or other loan in connection with the acquisition of an asset should not be treated as allowable expenditure (for capital gains tax purposes)." Furthermore, in HMRC's Property Income manual (tinyurl.com/kac9wuns) it states: "incidental costs incurred in obtaining loan finance for a rental business are generally deductible in computing rental business profits provided they relate wholly and exclusively to property let out on a commercial basis. These costs include loan fees, commissions, guarantee fees and fees in connection with the security of a loan." So, you can see that with regard to tax, the mortgage fee is not capitalised.

198. Transferring Property In Stages By Trust

Question: We want to transfer a buy-to-let property to our children by trust deed in stages, to complete the transfer in about ten years or longer, to save capital gains tax (CGT). I am 74 and my wife is 68. The property is valued at £1 million. There is no mortgage. It is held in our joint names. Will HMRC consider it as one transfer? What are the pros and cons of doing this?

Answer: If you look at HMRC's Capital Gains manual (tinyurl.com/ccz8uuce), you can see that HMRC calls this 'fragmentation' and does not like it. Furthermore, the disadvantages of doing so are: (a) as time goes on, it is likely that the value of the property will increase, and so the potential capital gain will also increase; and (b) in order to avoid the seven-year inheritance tax rule, it is necessary that you and your wife live seven years after the date of the gift, but this becomes harder if the gifts are spread over a number of years.

199. Selling Residential Property And Buying Another

Question: I let out my house to relocate and to live with my partner. I then bought another property to live in. Can I sell my rental and current residential property to buy a new residential property without incurring capital gains tax (CGT)?

Answer: There is no relief from CGT when selling a property in your circumstances, just because you are going to invest in a new residential property. The two scenarios where it could be applicable are when selling a furnished holiday letting property or in a situation of compulsory purchase.

200. Sell Both Properties As A Job Lot Or Separately?

Question: I have a large house, a very large garden and a holiday cottage within the garden. The cottage is rented out as a furnished holiday let. These are for sale as a job lot, or alternatively I am happy to split the title and sell at the same time, as two separate sales. What are the tax implications? I think there is 10% capital gains tax on the cottage only. Is this correct and is it the case no matter which way I sell?

Answer: The capital gains tax (CGT) rate for the house, garden and holiday cottage is 18% for a basic rate taxpayer and 28% for a higher rate taxpayer, because it is residential property. However, if you live in the house as your main residence, it is likely that a part (or even all) of the capital gain on the house and garden will be exempt due to principal private residence (PPR) relief.

As for the holiday cottage, it appears that you have not lived in it but only rented it out. If so, PPR relief will not be available. However, if this is the only property that you rent out as a furnished holiday letting, and if you fulfil the conditions for business asset disposal relief, you could be eligible for a 10% CGT rate.

201. What Would Be The CGT Position If We Pooled Our Property Resources?

Question: My wife and I both owned our own houses in our individual names before we began living together and subsequently married. I have owned mine since the 1980s, and she has owned her own since the 1990s.

We both still own the same two properties; neither is in joint names, and we do not intend to sell either house in the foreseeable future. The properties are each in different parts of England, one rural and the other suburban. Neither of them has ever been rented out to tenants. Their current combined value is approximately £600,000.

Answer: Since 1990, when independent taxation came in, each spouse is looked at independently of the other, so the assets that one spouse has will not impact on the other spouse. However, as far as principal private residence relief from capital gains tax is concerned, since you are now married (and I presume, living together), you will have to decide which house is your main residence. See HMRC's Capital Gains manual at CG64525 (tinyurl.com/y6h8ufas).

202. Moving Out And Removing My Name From The Mortgage

Question: I have recently split up with my ex-partner (we were not married), and I decided to move out of our house. We had a joint mortgage on the property. I decided to do a transfer of equity for £10,000 because my partner had put down the initial deposit on the house, and I didn't want to ask for any of that as I don't think that's right when it wasn't mine to begin with. My name has since been removed from the mortgage and from the land registry document. I had lived in the house ever since we bought it, and it was my main and only residence. I have seen some information online about capital gains tax (CGT) and now I am very worried that I might be liable.

Answer: From what you have written, it appears that until now, you owned half of the house, and now you have transferred your half to your ex-partner. If you had not lived in the house since you acquired your half as your only or main residence, this transfer would have triggered CGT. But since you did, you are eligible for principal private residence (PPR) relief, and you have no CGT to pay. You don't even need to report it on your self-assessment tax return because the entire gain is covered by PPR relief.

203. Are Any Taxes Due When We Sell Our Principal Home?

Question: My husband and I have owned a home for over twenty-five years, and it is our main residence. We file our taxes from there and all utilities are paid from there; we also vote from there. We rent a property in the countryside because our children's school is too far to commute, and most weekends and holidays we are at home. In the last few years, although not last year, we have periodically rented out the house through Airbnb. Our current mortgage is buy-to-let (BTL). It is our only home. Will we be liable for capital gain tax when we sell, even though it is our only property?

Answer: HMRC's Capital Gains manual at CG64500 states that where someone owns one house but also rents another property and lives concurrently in both, they can make an election that the house they own is their main residence and therefore, eligible for principal private residence relief, even if the election is made after the date it should have been made.

204. Do We Need To Report No Capital Gains Tax Due?

Question: We own a second property 50:50 and we are selling it for £98,000. As each share is below the 4x capital gains tax (CGT) limit and no CGT is due, does the sale still need to be reported to HMRC on completion?

Answer: HMRC's Capital Gains manual at CG10340, states as you have understood, that where the sales proceeds are less than 4 times the annual exemption (currently £12,300) and there is no CGT to pay, the taxpayer does not need to enter the sale on their self-assessment return. If there is no CGT to pay, the 60-day return after completion is not required.

205. What If I Move Into My Buy-To-Let Property And Then Sell?

Question: I have owned a buy-to-let property for 20 years. If I move back into it for two years as my sole property, do I need to pay capital gains tax (CGT) on it?

Answer: If you move back into the property for two years as your main residence and then sell it, having owned it for 22 years, you will be exempt from paying CGT, due to principal private residence (PPR) relief, only for the last two years. For example, if you bought it for £200,000 and sell it for £420,000, it has gone up by £10,000 a year. So, your PPR relief will be £20,000, but you will be taxable on £200,000.

206. CGT On Disposal Of Gifted Property: Which Price Do I Use?

Question: I was gifted my parents' house in April 2014 at a value of £150,000: 50% to my sister and 50% to me. Both parents are now deceased and we are putting the house up for sale; the guide price was £190,000-£210,000. Due to a family breakdown, my sister does not wish to receive the proceeds of the sale and is in the process of transferring her share to me so that I own the property 100% – this will shortly conclude. The house has been put up for sale and I have accepted an offer of £220,000.

I own my own property, so I will not qualify for principal private residence relief and I am aware both my sister and I will be treated as 'connected' persons. My sister's capital gains tax (CGT) gain will be, I assume, £75,000 to either £95,000 or £105,000 (half the guide price, as this would be adjudged market value) when she disposes or transfers her 50% share (for free). However, for CGT purposes when the house is actually sold, I am unsure what figure to use for my purchase price. Will the purchase price default to £150,000, or will it be £190,000 or £210,000?

Answer: Firstly, I would suggest that the current market price is not the guide price of £190,000-£210,000, but instead is £220,000 because you have a third-party purchaser who is willing to pay this. This market price should be used for transactions between you and your sister since you are connected persons, as you have written.

See HMRC's guidance in the Capital Gains manual, at https://tinyurl.com/2p8sf49p. So she is deemed to transfer to you at £110,000. At CG14530 it states, 'The same figure is used as the acquisition cost of the person who acquires the asset.' So you are making two sales. The original half, for which you have a base cost of £75,000, and the second half, for which you have a base cost of £110,000.'

207. When Selling Our Flat, Where Is The 'Factorial' Deducted From?

Question: Is the factorial paid over the period of tenure deductible from the selling price in calculating a net income in calculating capital gains tax?

Answer: The factorial is the Scottish term for the management company profit mark-up included in the management agreement.

208. Taxed On Sale Of The Whole Property Or Just A Quarter Share?

Question: My sister wants to sell her share of our holiday home in Torquay, which is owned as tenants-in-common in equal shares by my sister, myself, and our two brothers. She doesn't want us to buy her out for an agreed amount; she wants the whole house put on the market. Otherwise, she says she will take us to court for an Order for Sale. My question is about the tax implications of selling the whole house versus just a quarter share. If the house does go on the market and my brothers and I buy it, will we pay stamp duty land tax (SDLT) on the whole value of the house, even though we already own three-quarters of it? And will we, in addition, have to pay capital gains tax (CGT) on our own original shares which we will have (in a sense) bought from ourselves? Or (as I hope) will HMRC just be interested in the one-quarter share that is transferred from my sister to the other three owners, on which we will pay SDLT and she will pay CGT?

Answer: I think you need to get legal advice for this. However, although it is talking about something else, it states in HMRC's Business Income manual at BIM47820: 'This is because individuals cannot rent property to themselves.' I would suggest logic dictates that a person also cannot sell to themselves because a disposal means a change in ownership (see HMRC's Capital Gains manual at CG12700), and stamp duty land tax (SDLT) is charged on a land transaction, which is defined as 'the acquisition of a chargeable interest' (see HMRC's Stamp Duty Land Tax manual at SDLTM00260). So, it seems to me that you only need to concern yourself with SDLT and CGT on her quarter share.

209. When Will I Be Exempt From Paying CGT On Disposal Of My Property?

Question: I purchased a property in 2003 for £76,000. I am awaiting a valuation on it probably £120,000-£125,000). I lived in the property until 2008 as I fell ill during that time. I have had to evict my tenants this year (February 2022) and wish to return to the property. How long do I have to live in the property before it becomes free of capital gains tax (CGT) again? It will become my main home from February 2022, as I intend living in it again.

Answer: It is a common misconception that if you have owned a property for some years, and now move into it as your main residence, it can afterwards be sold free of CGT. The reality is that broadly you are exempt for the years you actually lived in it and are liable for the years you didn't live in it. In your case, let's say you move into it now, and live there until 2028, then sell. You will have then owned it for 25 years. You will broadly have to pay CGT on 14/25 of the gain and be exempt on 11/25 of the gain (this assumes that the 'period of absence' rules (see HMRC's Capital Gains manual at CG65040 and onwards) do not apply).

210. Tax Implications Of A Parent Transferring A Property Interest

Question: My father has a property in London, which he would like to jointly transfer into my name (50:50). What are the tax implications?

Answer: A transfer of a property from your father to you is deemed to take place at current market value for capital gains tax (CGT) purposes. So, if the property is worth more now than it was when he originally acquired it, he will have to pay CGT on 50% of the gain (see HMRC's Capital Gains manual at CG14530). If there is no change in responsibility for the mortgage, or if there is no mortgage on the property and if you are not paying your father anything, there will be no stamp duty land tax (SDLT) on this transfer. However, if there is 'consideration' for this transfer, there could be SDLT to pay.

211. Tax Implications Of Gifting Property To A Son

Question: My partner and I want to transfer a property to my son. It is our family home and mortgage-free.

If we stay in the property once we have gifted sole ownership to my son, will we have to pay rent at the full market rate (we are happy to do this)? Is it correct that if we are both alive for more than seven years post gifting the property, there will be no inheritance tax (IHT) for my son to pay on the house? Furthermore, if the property was to be gifted to my son, at what point do we pay capital gains tax (CGT) if he is now the owner and we just pay rent to live there? What will be the tax implications for my son, as he has been gifted the family home? Is he also able to then go to the bank and remortgage or obtain a mortgage for the property to use to build a portfolio or just have money in the bank to invest in whatever he thinks fit?

Answer: If you gift the property to your son but continue living in it, this will be a 'gift with reservation' and included in your estate when you die (i.e., you will not have achieved anything from an IHT perspective). You can overcome this by paying a market rent for living in it, for as long as you live in the property (see HMRC's Inheritance Tax manual at IHTM14341). If you do pay full market rent, then seven years after gifting the house, the gift will fall out of your estate and escape IHT. If you have lived in the house for all your period of ownership, you will be eligible for principal private residence relief from CGT when you transfer to your son. After the property has been gifted to your son, he can certainly attempt to get a mortgage on it.

212. Are Costs of Extending A Lease An Allowable Expense?

Question: I am selling a property which will have a sizeable capital gain (capital gains tax (CGT) will be approximately £100,000). At the same time as the exchange of contracts, I am planning to sell the benefit of a lease extension. The premium for the extension of 90 years is likely to be around £60,000 (I used a specialist surveyor for this – and the freeholder will, in turn, have a survey for which I will pay). My accountant tells me that the premium to extend the lease is a cost and is not an allowable expense for CGT purposes. But I have read elsewhere that it is an allowable expense. Also, are my expenses or costs of sale allowable expenses?

Answer: It appears from your question that you are a leaseholder of some land with X years to run on the lease. You are selling your leasehold rights to someone else. You are extending the lease by 90 years (by purchasing it from the freeholder), so you are selling a lease (of (X + 90 years) to the purchaser. This is enhancement expenditure (see HMRC's Capital Gains manual at CG15180) and an allowable expense in your CGT computation. Additionally, your costs of sale are an allowable expense (see CG15250).

213. What Are The Tax Implications Of Transferring Legal Title To My Property?

Question: I took out a second mortgage around 12 years ago to help my brother so he could buy out my other brother on a property in Manchester that they shared. At this time, I was living in my own mortgaged house and continued to do so until I sold it earlier this year (May). I now live in rented accommodation. I own the Manchester property in name only and have never lived there.

The mortgage payments were paid directly from his account, and I do not stand to make any profit on the transfer. I no longer wish to have the house in my name as it is potentially affecting my ability to get a mortgage and I would like to return it to him. I require advice on the best way to do this without attracting huge tax bills, etc. If the house is transferred to him, I understand there is a requirement to pay tax on profits as it's a second home, etc.

I've read that I may be able to gift the equity and he can take out a mortgage for the balance (£115,000) and pay stamp duty land tax on this amount. However, I'm just not sure, in particular about capital gains tax. My accountant and conveyancer have different ideas and are looking at it from different angles! The house was originally bought for £150,000 and is now worth circa £300,000 (maybe a bit more); the mortgage outstanding is £115,000.

Answer: From what you have described, it appears that you have simply been the legal owner or bare trustee nominee from day one, but your brother has been the beneficial owner all along; see HMRC's Capital Gains manual at CG70230.

If so, I suggest you ask your solicitor to draw up a declaration of trust showing that this has been the case since 2010 (see HMRC's Trusts, Settlements and Estates manual at TSEM9520). When this is in place, it is a simple matter to change the legal ownership from you to your brother, and there should be no capital gains tax consequences (see CG12704 and CG10720). However, the mortgage will need to be dealt with.

214. Purchase Lease Option And Minimising Tax Liabilities

Question: I am a new property investor, and I am looking at a property where the owner is willing to give me a five-year purchase lease option (PLO) for £550,000. Whilst this PLO is great for me, I do not know if giving me this PLO will disadvantage her from a tax perspective when we complete in five years. This is her primary residence and from what I understand, private residence relief (PRR) only applies for nine months after she moves out. After that, I imagine she could be charged capital gains tax (CGT) on the £200,000 of gain she has accumulated. Can this tax liability be managed to minimise the impact on her?

Answer: From what you have written, I assume that you have an option to purchase the property by 2027 at today's market value of £550,000 but that you expect the property to have a market value of £750,000 by the time you purchase. The seller is planning to move out so that you can rent out the property to someone else. If so, you are correct that the seller is at a disadvantage because they will only get private residence relief from CGT until the date they move out, plus a further nine months final period exemption. The remainder will be subject to CGT. However, you must bear in mind that you have no guarantee that the property will increase in value to £750,000.

215. What Would Be The Most Tax-Efficient Way Of Disposing Of Half A Property?

Question: My younger brother and I equally own a buy-to-let house. I would like to sell it, but he would not, and he would like to take over my 50% share. At the moment, he is not financially stable but he could easily afford the interest-only repayments of the £400,000 mortgage. It is valued at around £700,000 and was purchased for £360,000. Personally, I would have to pay the higher rate of capital gains tax (CGT) and if I could gift it to my brother, my parents have agreed to pay me cash, so I would not be out of pocket. What do you think is the best way forward?

Answer: If you trust your brother, you could sell to him now and wait for him to pay you. You could get the solicitor to draw up a proper legal agreement, giving you a charge on the property until you are paid in full. Or maybe your parents could guarantee the sale, or even pay you now, similar to what you yourself have written. However, because he is your brother, even if you gift it to him for no consideration, you are deemed to sell to him at today's market value of £700,000 for CGT purposes, so you will be making a large capital gain. This is unavoidable.

216. CGT Relief On Extending A Lease?

Question: My husband and I own a flat in a council-owned building. We extended the existing lease. We are now gifting the flat to our son. Can we include: (1) the money we paid to the council (freeholder) as a cost in our capital gains tax (CGT) calculation; and (2) the cost of the professional company that did all the paperwork and negotiation with the freeholder to extend the lease?

Answer: (1) You can claim the cost you paid to the council (freeholder) as a cost in your CGT calculation. This goes for the original purchase of the flat and also for the extension of the lease (see HMRC's guidance at tinyurl.com/2p99h25x) although, there, it discusses the subsequent purchase of the freehold), (2) See HMRC's Property Income manual at tinyurl.com/2p92uxar, which states: 'The normal legal and professional fees incurred on the renewal of a lease are also allowable if the lease is for less than 50 years.' This implies that if the lease extension is for more than 50 years, the costs involved are capital in nature.

217. Sale Of Second Home: What Is The CGT Position?

Question: We are a retired married couple and have lived in our present home for 38 years. We bought a second home in November 2002 to retire there but we never did fully live there. We paid £185,000, and it is now worth around £400,000. We have been thinking of moving to our second home but if we didn't like living there, moving back to our old home. We have been told if we lived in our second home for nine months and changed everything to that address, we would be capital gains tax free. Could you advise us if this is the best way?

Answer: Unfortunately, you have been wrongly advised. If you move now to your second home for nine months and make it your main residence, then sell it, you will only get proportional relief from capital gains tax. Let's say you sell it in May 2023 for £400,000, having owned it for 20.5 years. Your capital gain of (£400,000 - £185,000) = £215,000 equates to a gain of £10,488 per year, which equates to £7,866 for nine months. So, your chargeable gain will be £215,000 less £7,866 principal private residence relief = £207,134.

218. Owner-Occupied For Part Of Ownership Period

Question: I bought a property in May 1979 and worked there as self-employed until January 1987. I rented it out, and it has been rented since then. I believe the property would have been valued at £40,000 in 1985. At present, it is rented out and is valued at £300,000. What capital gains tax (CGT) will I have to pay, and is any relief available as it was used as an owner-occupied business for some time?

Answer: Firstly, it is the March 1982 value that is important, not the 1985 value. Let's say it was worth £30,000 in 1982. If it is sold today for £300,000, your capital gain will be (£300,000 - £30,000) = £270,000. For just over 40 years, between March 1982 and now, this equates to an approximate capital gain of £6,750 per year. It is not clear what kind of business use you occupied the house for.

Let us make an assumption (rightly or wrongly) that your business use did not prejudice your principal private residence (PPR) relief. If so, you are eligible for PPR relief for the first 58 months you lived there (i.e., April 1982 to January 1987) (see HMRC's Capital Gains manual at CG64940) plus the last nine months of ownership, called the final period exemption (i.e., 21 December to 22 August = 67 months). At a rate of £6,750 per year, you are eligible for PPR relief of £37,688 for 67 months. That means your chargeable capital gain is £270,000 - £37,688 = £232,312.

219. Will I Have To Pay Capital Gains Tax?

Question: I currently own two residential properties. Property 1 was purchased by myself 16 years ago and was where I lived. Two years later, I got married and purchased a second residential property with my wife, which we both moved into, and it became our main residence (under joint ownership). I kept property 1 for my mother to stay in rent-free. If I decide to sell property 2 (my main residence) and move back to property 1, will I pay any capital gains tax (CGT) in the future (e.g., in five to ten years) if I decide to sell property 1? I want to know whether, should you sell your main residence CGT-free and then move into your second property so that it becomes your main and only property residence, you still have to pay CGT on it if you sell it in (say) ten years' time.

Answer: I presume that you did not make any election or nomination for which house should be your principal private residence (PPR). See HMRC's guidance in its Capital Gains manual at CG64545 (https://tinyurl.com/bdzz53nu). It appears that property 1 was your main residence from 2006 to 2008, and then property 2 became your main residence from 2008 to 2022. If you sell property 2 now, you will have no CGT liability because all the capital gain will be exempt due to PPR relief. If you then move back to property 1, make it your main residence, and then sell it in (say) 2026, having owned it for 20 years, you will be subject to paying CGT on (14/20) of the capital gain (for the 14 years that property 1 was not your PPR), and you will be exempt from paying CGT on (6/20) of the capital gain (for the six years you actually lived in the property).

220. Gift Of Property: What Base Cost Should I Use?

Question: A client gifted a property to their daughter, which she has since been renting out. She is now considering selling the property, which is not her main residence. In calculating any potential capital gains tax (CGT) liability, what figure should be used as the base cost to be deducted from any disposal proceeds?

Answer: The figure to use for the daughter's base cost on the sale of this property is the market value of the property on the date the parent gifted it to the daughter. See the end of the first paragraph in HMRC's Capital Gains manual at CG14530.

221. What Are The Tax Implications If Half Of The Property Is Transferred

Into My Name?

Question: My husband and his brother ran a pub for 33 years. They have now both retired and are drawing their pensions. We live in the third floor flat and the brother and his wife live in the second floor flat over the pub, which was on the ground floor; this has now been cleared out and is awaiting planning permission for residences. The brother is the sole owner of the entire building. He wants to transfer half of the entire building into my husband's name so that when it is sold, they each get half of the profit. What tax implications will my husband have? The property is valued at approximately £600,000.

Answer: When the brother transfers half the building into your husband's name, for capital gains tax (CGT) purposes it will be treated in the same way as though he had sold it to someone at market value. Two brothers are 'connected persons', so the market rule applies. See HMRC's Capital Gains manual at CG14530. So even though, in actuality, it is a gift for no payment as far as the CGT rules are concerned, the brother will be deemed to have sold it to your husband for £300,000.

222. Should The Property Be Transferred To Me?

Question: My husband and I have been amicably separated for over two years since he moved out of our home. His name is on the title deeds and he pays the mortgage. We are looking at selling our house but he has a six-figure IRS tax bill in the US, and our worry is that the taxman will take the money from the sale of the house to pay it, leaving me with nothing.

He is a broadcaster and created a limited company for his earnings at the request of his employer. The IRS found him liable to pay them backdated taxes. I haven't worked for ten years but my husband pays me £2,000 to £3,000 a month. His priority is that I should come out of the sale of the home with enough money to buy myself a small house or flat outright to ensure my future is secure. We are not sure if I should try to take over the mortgage and have the deeds transferred into my name or if there are other options.

Answer: By 'IRS', I presume you mean the US Internal Revenue Service and not HMRC. From a UK tax perspective, if your husband transfers the house to you, there will be no UK capital gains tax (CGT) consequences. If you take on responsibility for the mortgage, you will have to pay stamp duty land tax (SDLT) based on the amount of the mortgage but if your husband retains responsibility for the mortgage, you won't. However, how the IRS will view this 'deprivation of capital', and whether they come after you because your husband recently transferred his house to you, I cannot answer.

223. What Taxes Will Be Payable On Gifted Property?

Question: My father is considering gifting the property in London that my partner and I, and our children are currently living in. My father is non-UK domiciled, and both my partner and I are resident in the UK.

We would like to know:

1. What taxes are liable (for all parties) if my father gifts the property to me?

2. What taxes are liable (for all parties) if my father gifts the property to me and my partner?
3. What taxes are liable (for all parties) if the property is gifted to me and, subsequently, I decide to share ownership or equity in the property with my partner?

Answer: In all cases, your father will be liable to capital gains tax (CGT) if the current market value of the property is more than what he paid for the property. If he is not UK resident (not the same definition as 'non-UK domiciled'), he will be liable to UK CGT on the increase in value from April 2015 onwards only. If there is no mortgage on the property, so no transfer of responsibility for the mortgage, there will be no stamp duty land tax for you (the recipients) to pay.

If, soon after receiving the property as a gift, you share ownership with your partner, there should be no CGT for you to pay. The reason is that when you receive it, you are deemed (for CGT purposes) to have paid market value for it, so if you transfer it (or half of it) to your partner soon afterwards, it will not have increased in value (or hardly increased), hence no CGT. See HMRC's Capital Gains Manual.

224. How Can We Minimise Our Tax Liabilities when we sell?

Question: My wife owns a five-bedroom flat in London, which she inherited from her Aunt in 2012. The property was worth £315,000 in 2012, but she has since purchased the two servants' quarters in the loft, and the price is now £650,000. This is her second home, as my wife and I have joint ownership of our family home, where we have lived for 18 years. Is there any way she can avoid paying 28% capital gains tax (CGT) between when we sell later this year at a value of £650,000 and the value when she inherited it of £315,000 in 2012 (so, £335,000 @ 28% = £93,800)? The flat has been rented since 2012.

Answer: Whilst the sale proceeds may well now be £650,000, and the acquisition cost was the probate value in 2012 of £315,000, that does not mean that the capital gain is £335,000. After the inheritance, your wife paid a sum of money (I presume) to purchase the two servants' quarters in the loft. This is allowable expenditure for CGT purposes. So, suppose she spent £100,000; her resultant taxable gain would be £235,000. Furthermore, incidental costs when purchasing the loft quarters and when selling the flat are also allowable expenses. See HMRC's Capital Gains manual at CG15250. In addition, your wife may have her annual exempt amount (£6,000 for 2023/24) available to reduce her capital gain.

225. Boiler change – Improvement for CGT purposes?

Question: I am selling a second property, which has been rented out. I am aware that I will be subject to capital gains tax. It was a new build when I bought it 15 years ago so it didn't need any improvements except that last year, we changed the boiler to a condensing type which is around 30% more efficient. Could this be claimed as an improvement? Can I use this to offset the gain?

Answer: If you look at HMRC's Property Income Manual at PIM2030 in the section headed 'When there is capital improvement' it states: 'It is largely a question of fact and degree in each case whether expenditure on a property leads to an improvement. Sometimes the improvement may be so small as to count as incidental to a repair. In the absence of other capital indications, the entire cost is then revenue expenditure. Problems can arise where the customer does work on an old asset.

A repair or replacement of a part of a building using modern materials may give an apparent element of improvement because of the greater durability, superior qualities and so forth of the new material. But the cost normally remains revenue expenditure where any improvement arises only because the customer uses new materials that are broadly equivalent to the old materials. For example, the following are usually revenue expenses in the absence of any other capital indications.

The cost of replacing: wooden beams with steel girders, and lead pipes with copper or plastic pipes. There is likely to be capital expenditure if, say, the steel girders were designed to take heavier loads so that the building could take larger machines after the work was done. The same is true if the new pipes are designed to take greater pressure or heat.

But there is usually no improvement if trivial increases in performance or capacity arise solely from the replacement of old materials with newer but broadly equivalent materials. For example, the replacement of pipes or storage tanks of imperial measure with the closest metric equivalent may result in slightly increased diameter or capacity but the cost is still revenue expenditure.

Alterations due to advancements in technology are generally treated as an allowable repair rather than an improvement, if the functionality and character of the asset is broadly the same. For example, when single glazing is replaced with double glazing.'

226. Any Tax If I gift My Share Of Property To Sibling?

Question: I share ownership of a small rural property in Scotland with my sibling, who lives in and owns the main house on whose land the small property stands. Am I able to simply gift my half to them or are there tax implications? I am resident in France for tax purposes.

Answer: If you gift your half of the property to your sibling, it is deemed to be transferred at today's market value. If this is higher than the value when you acquired your share, you will be subject to capital gains tax (CGT) on the difference. You state that you are resident in France for tax purposes. Since you are non-UK resident, the capital gain will only be calculated on the increase in value from April 2015 until now for residential property, and from April 2019 until now for non-residential property.

227. Tax Implications Of Equity Transfer?

Question: My wife and I had our house converted into two flats in 2008. We own both flats; my wife and I live downstairs, and our son lives upstairs. We plan on doing an equity transfer of the upstairs flat to our son, so he will be the sole owner. We would like to know what the capital gains tax position would be upon the transfer.

Answer: Please see HMRC's Capital Gains Tax Manual at CG65271. It explains there that you look at the total value of the two separate flats on the date of the transfer or sale ('A'). Then you look at the value of the unconverted house on the date of the transfer or sale ('B'). A - B = the total capital gain ('C'). C has to be apportioned between the two flats proportionate to their value. For example, if flat 1 is worth 40% of A, and flat 1 is the one transferred, then 40% of C is the capital gain on the transfer of flat 1.

228. Renovating And Selling Our Home: What Is The Tax Position?

Question: Following an inheritance, I am able to purchase a new property outright whilst living in our current home, which is still currently mortgaged. The new property will be our main place of residence, but only after light renovations are completed on the current house in readiness for sale. We would continue to live in and pay the mortgage until it is sold and the mortgage settled. Under the circumstances, would we be liable to pay any capital gains tax (CGT)?

Answer: If you have lived in your current house as your main residence all the period of your ownership, principal private residence relief will mean no CGT on its sale. However, if you have only lived in it as your main residence for part of your period of ownership, in very simple terms the CGT relief will be in proportion to the period it was your main residence.

229. The Most Tax-Efficient Way To Transfer Equity

Question: If I (a non-UK resident) transfer to my daughter (a UK resident who is living in the flat) 50% equity of the flat I purchased in 2021 for around £270,000 (which is not under a mortgage) for no consideration, will she or I be liable for capital gains tax (CGT)? If so, would it be better from a tax perspective to bequeath the flat to her under my will, in which case there will be no inheritance tax (IHT) payable, given the threshold of £500,000 for gifts to children?

Answer: If the flat is worth more today than it was in 2021, you will be subject to CGT on half the value of the house (e.g., if today the flat is worth £350,000, you will be deemed to be making a capital gain of £40,000. It is true that there is a nil-rate band for IHT purposes of £325,000 and a residence nil-rate band (RNRB) of £175,000 if the person's main residence is left to their children, so totalling £500,000. However, you should clarify with a tax adviser whether you are eligible for the RNRB.

230. Can Lease Renewal Costs Be Claimed?

Question: Can I claim the cost of renewing the lease on a second property for capital gains tax (CGT) purposes when I sell the property?

Answer: Simply put, the cost of renewing a lease is capital expenditure and, as such, will be allowable expenditure in a CGT computation. However, a short lease (i.e., with less than 50 years to run) is a 'wasting asset' and so is subject to special rules.

Inheritance Tax

232. Inheritance Tax Planning - Which Is The Best Way?

Question: Whilst reading your December 2013 edition of the Property Tax Insider magazine, there is mention relating to inheritance tax planning and the fact that there are differences between whether a rental business generates investment property income or trading income. Can you please elaborate to what benefits each has and what can be done in the accounts to show that you are a majority of one and not the other?

Answer: If a rental business is classified as trading it should be eligible for business property relief from inheritance tax. It should also be eligible for rollover relief from capital gains tax for replacement of business assets. However, Class 2 and 4 National Insurance contributions must be paid on trading income. More important than what is shown in the accounts is the level of services provided with the accommodation. Letting furnished accommodation with extra services provided is investment income, whereas running a hotel is trading income. The distinction can sometimes be a narrow one.

233. Is There A Tax Efficient Way To Make Gifts?

Question: What are the implications where parents make regular (monthly) financial gifts to their adult 'children' and is there a tax efficient way to make such gifts?

Answer: A gift from a parent to a child is a potentially exempt transfer (PET) as far as Inheritance Tax (IHT) is concerned. If the parent survives seven years after the gift, it will be disregarded as far as IHT is concerned.

However, if it is a regular small amount, it is likely to fall under the 'Normal expenditure out of income' rules, in which case it is exempt from IHT and is not a PET. To fall under these rules, the gift must be 'part of your normal expenditure, and must not, taking one year with another, reduce your available net income (after all other transfers) below that required to maintain your usual standard of living'.

The following may be possible: the parent could gift a proportion of a property to the child, e.g. 10% of a buy to let property that they are receiving rental income from. If the child is over 18, for tax purposes, it will be the child's income.

Since only 10% is being gifted, maybe there will not be any CGT on the transfer, because the gain is covered by the annual exemption. The income will be taxed on the child, instead of the parent, thus saving income tax.

234. How Do I Minimise My Children's IHT On A Property?

Question: How do I minimise my children's inheritance tax on a property, whilst continuing to own that property during my lifetime?

Answer: It is not possible to avoid IHT on a residential property while continuing to own it. However:

if it is commercial property used in the taxpayer's business, it may qualify for Business Property Relief from IHT, and if not, it may be possible to put the property into a discretionary trust, which would take the property out of the estate of the taxpayer, while still allowing them a degree of control (i.e. as a trustee).

Consequently, if it is sold soon after death by the inheritor/recipient, there should be no CGT to pay because, presumably, it should be worth the same as it was when the original owner died. However, if it has gone up in value the inheritor/recipient will have made a capital gain. They will, of course, be able to use their capital gains tax annual exemption to reduce the amount on which they are liable to capital gains tax.

Just because it is your second property is not a reason for you to pay more/extra CGT or be the victim of another tax charge. However, you will not have the benefit of the principal private residence relief from capital gains tax of your first property (the property in which you live).

235. Using Property Gifted To My Son?

Question: A deed of gift was finalised on 20 January 2023 and the title deeds were changed into my son's name. I have stayed in the property to sort out my move for two months only. Are there any consequences or implications in doing that? I intend to move out of the gifted property immediately.

Answer: When you transfer to your son, this is a potentially exempt transfer for inheritance tax (IHT) purposes. However, if you continue to benefit from the property (e.g., you continue to live in it), it is still included in your estate for IHT purposes because it is a 'gift with reservation' (GWR). When you stop benefiting from it, the seven-year 'clock' starts because the GWR has ceased. See HMRC's Inheritance Tax Manual at IHTM04072 ('Reservation ceasing in transferor's lifetime').

236. Can My Mother Live Rent-Free?

Question: My Mother is thinking of buying a retirement property which would be her main residence. She will sell the family home which she owns and presently occupies on her own.

My question is can my Mother give away the proceeds of the sale to her 3 children, and then live rent free in the retirement property which would be purchased and owned by 1 or more of her children. She has other assets in excess of the IHT threshold and has sufficient income to live on.

Answer: Your mother can certainly do so. The only question is what would be the taxation consequences? The gift to the 3 children would be a potentially exempt transfer (PET) as far as Inheritance Tax is concerned. Since the mother has given the sale proceeds to the child, who then goes and purchases property that the mother lives in, it would probably fall into the Pre-Owned Asset regime by virtue of Finance Act 2004 Chapter 15 paragraph 3.

The family should consider putting the property into trust, which has certain taxation advantages in this scenario. However, professional advice is essential to do this properly.

237. If I Die Will IHT Be Due Immediately?

Question: If have an estate worth £400,000. If I was to die tomorrow the estate would be passed to my children. Would they be liable to pay IHT immediately, which may mean that they have to sell the primary residence to pay the IHT bill?

Answer: If the deceased person's estate does not consist entirely of property then generally speaking IHT is due immediately. However, if the estate does consist of only property then it is possible to pay any IHT liability over a 10-year period.

238. How Can I Avoid Inheritance Tax?

Question: How can I plan to avoid inheritance tax?

Answer: The single most cost-effective way to avoid IHT is to give away assets and hope to survive for seven years!

However, most people don't wish to do so for three reasons:

- they still want to benefit from the assets themselves,
- they don't trust the recipients, and
- a capital gain can often be triggered when gifting assets.

A discretionary trust can sometimes help to overcome b) and c).

Another effective way of avoiding IHT is to convert one's property into qualifying business assets which are 100% exempt from IHT. These are basically an interest in a trade (a sole trade or a partnership) or shares in a trading company that have been owned for two years. However, investments and shares in an investment company do not qualify.

A similar 100% exemption applies to qualifying agricultural property.

A not so commonly known method of avoidance is relevant to people with large amounts of regular annual income, some of which they don't use. If they get into the habit of giving away a proportion of their income every year while still maintaining their normal lifestyle, then even if they don't survive for seven years, this will fall out of their IHT computation.

239. What Is The Tax Position For A Settlor And Trustee?

Question: Is it possible to create a property trust whereby the settlor adds a buy-to-let property to a trust and the property in the trust is not considered an asset of the settlor, but at the same time the settlor receives rental income from the trust? What are the tax implications for the settlor and for the trustees please?

Answer: The property in a discretionary Trust is not considered an asset of the settlor, for inheritance tax (IHT) purposes. If the settlor is also a beneficiary of the discretionary trust the trustees have a right, and the discretion, to pay the rental income to the settlor. However, this arrangement is not so tax-efficient, because the trust income is taxed at 45% (the trust rate), and the assets within the trust are subject to the IHT exit charge and ten-year-charge rules.

240. Transferring Property From Sole To Joint Ownership - Any Pitfalls?

Question: I own my property, unencumbered, and it has a value of around £300,000. I am single and share my house with a friend of some 35 years standing and who is 18 years my junior. To protect his position I am keen to transfer my property to our joint names, but am concerned as to the cost of doing so in terms of tax and/or stamp duty. My estate today is about £750,000 and I would like to Will my share of the house to him. I am 71 and hope to be around for another seven years, and to protect my position would expect my friend to prepare a Will leaving his share to me should he predecease me. Apart from the costs referred to above, are there any other pitfalls that I should take into account?

Answer: Even though you mentioned 'I would Will my share', nevertheless from the rest of your question it is evident that you intend to make a lifetime gift of half your home to your partner. Since it is your main residence, there is no capital gains tax on the transfer. Since you are gifting for no consideration, there is no stamp duty land tax. With regard to Inheritance tax, if you continue to live in the house, it is a gift with reservation, and you will not have succeeded in taking £150,000 out of your estate, liable to IHT.

However, if you look at page IHTM14332 (paragraph e)) of HMRC's inheritance tax manual, you can see that if your partner pays his share of the running costs while both of you live in the property at the same time, then it will not be a 'gift with reservation', and if you live for seven years after making the gift you will have succeeded in taking £150,000 out of your estate, saving £60,000 in IHT.

241. Mum Gave Me Gift Of House But Died Within Seven Years

Question My mum died before the seven years were up (six years and three months) after she transferred the title deeds of a house into my name. What will happen now for inheritance tax purposes?

Answer: The gift of the house by your mother uses up part or all of inheritance tax nil rate band of £325,000 that was available to her estate. So more of the remaining estate will now not be covered by the nil rate band, and therefore subject to inheritance tax. If the value of the house when transferred was more than the nil rate band, extra tax on the house will have to be paid now, but 80% taper relief (more than six years since date of death) would be available against the extra tax.

242. Would Rented-Out Property Be Classed As PPR For IHT Purposes?

Question My brother is in a care home, and he wishes to use the funds from the sale of his large home to purchase a house to rent out. Would this property be classed as his one residence for inheritance tax purposes and am I right in thinking the allowance will go up on 1 April 2017 by £100,000 if you have only one residence?

Answer: See www.gov.uk/government/case-studies/inheritance-tax-residence-nil-rate-band-case-studies at case study 16. Depending on the figures involved it could be that your brother will be eligible for the new downsizing rules and benefit from the new residence nil rate band.

243. What Are The Tax Implications??

Question I own a property in the Midlands, which is worth about £500,000. The outstanding mortgage is £240,000. Can I gift this property entirely to my brother-in-law, and if so what are the tax implications on me and him?

Answer: There are no direct implications on your brother-in-law (except that: (a) his estate will be increased by £500,000 for inheritance tax (IHT) purposes; and (b) if he now wants to purchase a residential property, he will have to pay an extra 3% stamp duty land tax because it will be his second property). The tax implications on you are: (a) if the property was worth less than £500,000 when you acquired it, you will have to pay capital gains tax on the difference; and (b) if you do not live for seven years after the date of the gift, the £500,000 will be included in your estate for IHT purposes.

244. Have We Left Ourselves Exposed to IHT?

Question As an unmarried couple, we bought our existing property 16 years ago. Whilst I contributed a large capital sum towards the purchase, the property was taken out in my partner's name only, as she was transferring an existing mortgage and I was starting up a business with irregular income. We are now unencumbered. We are both in the throes of making out mirror wills, leaving all our assets to the other (or to our 17-year-old son, if she or I pre-decease the other). I now realise that both my son and I are very much tax exposed and may well have to sell our home in order to pay inheritance tax, if his mother should die before I do. I would welcome your advice as to the best course of action to take in order to rectify the situation.

Answer: Your partner could transfer half the house to you now. There would be no capital gains tax on this transfer because it would be covered by principal private residence relief. If she lived for seven years after the gift, there would be inheritance tax on the transfer. Alternatively, you could decide to get married now. Thirdly, maybe you want to consider discussing the matter with a tax adviser and maybe he could establish whether you have half the beneficial ownership in the property as per HMRC's guidance at www.gov.uk/hmrc-internal-manuals/capital-gains-manual/cg70230, www.gov.uk/hmrc-internal-manuals/capital-gains-manual/cg22020, and www.gov.uk/hmrc-internal-manuals/capital-gains-manual/cg65310 (although these last two discuss spouses).

245. Can I Gift Sale Proceeds To My Wife?

Question: I have sold a property on 31 Jan 2020 that was solely on my name. Is there any way that I can assign/gift (say) £12,000 of capital gains to my wife now so that she too can take advantage of my capital gains tax (CGT) allowance?

Answer: Unfortunately, no. Once the sale has been made, there is no way that you can make use of your wife's CGT annual exemption.

246. Transfer Of Mother's Home: Any Inheritance Tax (IHT) Pitfalls?

Question: My mother is 94 and has decided to transfer her home into my name. This is already written in her will. I know her home has to be valued and she has to have a capability test by a GP. We enquired about a year ago. The results are to be submitted to a solicitor to carry on with transfer. What I need to know is whether there is a threshold for IHT? Apart from her house, she has no other assets.

Answer: IHT will only be applicable when she dies, not now at the time of the gift to you (it is a potentially exempt transfer (PET)). From what you have described, quite likely she will be eligible for the residence nil rate band (RNRB) of £175,000, in addition to the regular nil rate band (NRB) of £325,000. So if her house is worth £500,000 or less, there will be no IHT. However, there are other factors to take into account (e.g. (a) Whether any other gifts to individuals (PETs) are made in the seven years before she dies; (b) Did she inherit any NRB or RNRB from her husband?) (c) Is she continuing to live in the house after gifting it to you? in which case it will be a gift with reservation).

247. **Transferring beneficial interest: What is the tax position?**

    Question: I own two properties in my name and one jointly with my wife, all in Manchester. The properties have buy-to-let (BTL) mortgages. I have recently returned to work. I was wondering about transferring the beneficial interest to my wife for all three properties. My main concerns are that I do not want to inform the lender (I believe from the mortgage T&Cs I do not have to, but these would need checking) and I want to understand any stamp duty land tax (SDLT) or other tax implications so I can get a full cost picture.

    Answer: I cannot comment on what you write about the lenders; but let us make an assumption for the moment that you are fine as far as the mortgage companies are concerned. There is no capital gains tax when one spouse transfers to another spouse with whom they are living together. If you continue to be responsible for the mortgages, as you were before the transfers, then assuming you transfer to your wife as a gift for no consideration – there will be no SDLT implications. You need to contact a solicitor to provide you with a suitable 'declaration of trust'. Or perhaps look at https://www.litrg.org.uk/tax-guides/savers-property-owners-and-other-tax-issues/introduction-trusts/do-i-need-register-my by the Low Incomes Tax Reform Group about registering a non-taxable bare trust with the HMRC Trust Registration Service.

For more tax saving strategies please visit: **www.taxinsider.co.uk**

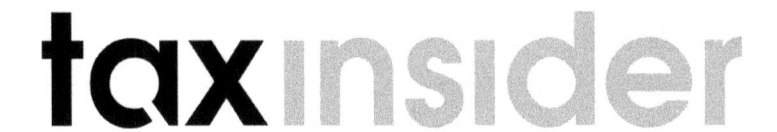

taxinsider

If you want to get better organised with landlord software that runs 'in the cloud' then visit: **www.landlordvision.co.uk**

landlord vision

Congratulations – You've now finished '247 Property Tax Questions Answered'
To learn even more ways on how to legitimately cut your property tax bills please visit: www.property-tax-portal.co.uk.